Tomorrow's World

Tomorrow's World

A Look at the Demographic and Socio-Economic Structure of the World in 2032

Clint Laurent

WILEY

Other Wiley Editorial Offices
John Wiley & Sons, 111 River Street, Hoboken, NJ 07030, USA
John Wiley & Sons, The Atrium, Southern Gate, Chichester, West Sussex, P019 8SQ, United Kingdom
John Wiley& Sons (Canada) Ltd., 5353 Dundas Street West, Suite 400, Toronto, Ontario, M9B 6HB, Canada
John Wiley& Sons Australia Ltd., 42 McDougall Street, Milton, Queensland 4064, Australia
Wiley-VCH, Boschstrasse 12, D-69469 Weinheim, Germany

ISBN 978-0-470-82471-9 (Cloth)
ISBN 978-0-470-82916-5 (ePDF)
ISBN 978-0-470-82915-8 (Mobi)
ISBN 978-0-470-82917-2 (ePub)

Typeset in 11.5/14 pt. Bembo Std. by MPS Limited, Chennai, India.
Printed in Singapore by Markono Print Media Pte Ltd.

10 9 8 7 6 5 4 3 2 1

Contents

Acknowledgments

There are a number of individuals whom I would like to thank for their contribution to this work. First, of course, my wife, Carol, who encouraged me to do and complete this. The encouragement was and is appreciated. I also must thank Amy Yam and Jessica Tsang, my colleagues in Global Demographics Ltd., who played a significant role in developing the database that underlies this work. Finally, thanks to Michael Sorkin for his critical review—it helped keep things in perspective.

Introduction

The nature of this book requires that this introduction set up parameters in terms of what it will cover, sources of information, and potential bias in interpretation. This understanding of these issues from the outset will avoid questions later and help the reader gain maximum value from the subsequent discussion.

Why Demographics?

Probably the most important point to address at the outset of this book is, "Why even look at future demographic trends?" After all, while we all get older, one year at a time, doesn't the overall picture remain relatively stable in nature? The answer is clearly no (although we do get older one year at a time—sorry, can't change that!). With changes in birth rates, death rates, social attitudes, education, and the very nature of the economy, the actual profile of the population of each country and region changes quite significantly, and in a relatively short period of time, as do the growth dynamics. For example, it might surprise you to hear that overall, for the regions and countries covered in this book, the fastest growing age group for the next 20 years is 64 plus, not the young; already, in many parts of the world, the 40 to 64 year age group is more significant in size, and has far greater absolute value and growth in spending power than the youth segments. So much for the marketing advice that is given so often, namely, "Target the young affluent." The young affluent group is becoming a minority segment and is not the growth opportunity of the next decade. Yet so many company strategies are focused on this segment because the nature of the present is believed to be the future.

Examining the changing pattern of demographics is very important in identifying future opportunities for business, as well as for the individual, to understand how the world is changing around them. Fortunately, it can be done with quite a high degree of reliability. Most demographic trends and relationships are quite stable in nature; that is, the year-on-year values of the key drivers of demographic change—births by age of mother, deaths by age and gender—follow a consistent trend over time, whatever that trend might be. True, they move above and below the line on a year-by-year basis but, overall, the trend is followed. This means it is possible to gain a quite reliable picture of the nature of the consumer in next 10 to 20 years as a result of the collective impact of these trends. This, in turn, enables firms to develop new products or services which will meet the needs of the new consumer profiles that will become important in the future. Similarly, governments, and society in general can plan for the needs of the new society, which might include increasing demand for health care or education. Consider, for example, the reality of the change in the composition of the average household. A decade ago it was more likely to have at least one person under the age of 19 in it than not. In just ten years, the opposite is going to be true—the majority of households in the 74 countries covered in this book will be childless. This will have significantly implications for the type of housing sought, demand for education services, the type and amount of products sought and, ultimately, the growth in demand for services and experiences.

By expressly examining the changes that take place it helps avoid certain myths becoming perceived truths, which in turn influence the interpretation of events in the world or business strategies. Two examples of this follow: The first is that China needs to keep growing its total real GDP in order keep its growing working-age population employed. The reality is that China's working-age population (defined as persons between the ages of 15 and 64, inclusive) peaked in 2010 and is now declining, a reality recognised by the Chinese government itself. Yet frequently one reads articles making this statement concerning China's need to grow its GDP. Second, that Japan has a major sociological problem emerging as its population is biased to older persons and it will not have enough workers to support them. Yet currently Japan has one of the lowest dependency ratios (number of persons supported by each employed person) in the world and will continue to do so for the next 20 years—its dependency ratio is one third of that of India— and yet no one says India has a similar problem!

One of the major objectives of this book—and hence an answer to the question "Why demographics?"—is to give readers a reasonably reliable quantitative base from which to understand the world. They can then overlay that base with their own interpretation of its implications for social, and even political, change.

Regions Rather than Countries

Because the purpose of this book is to give the reader an insight into the dominant trends that are emerging in terms of demographic profiles, the distribution of household by income, and expenditure patterns, it is important that it be done in a way that makes the picture comprehensible. This means there has to be some degree of data aggregation and summary. The data underlying this book provide a database for each of 74 countries, and if the analysis was reported at a country level it frankly would become confusing. There would be too much detail and not enough meaning. In short, to use the old phrase, there is a risk that you, the reader, would not see the forest for the trees.

So, the decision was made to group countries by region. While there are many obvious examples of the exception to the rule, overall countries in the same region tend to have similar demographic profiles and levels of affluence. This means that we have been able to reduce the results of the analysis to seven regions. Two of these regions are countries, India and China, but as each of these accounts for over 20 percent of the world's total population they are, individually, larger in terms of population than most regions, and hence warrant special attention.

Another exception to this regional grouping is Asia. Excluding China and India there are two groups of countries in the broad Asia region. There are the affluent and older countries (Hong Kong, Singapore, Japan, South Korea, Taiwan, Macau, Australia, and New Zealand) and the younger and poorer (Malaysia, Indonesia, Thailand, Philippines, Vietnam, Cambodia, Sri Lanka, Pakistan, and Bangladesh). So, while they overlap geographically, they have nonetheless been treated as separate regions.

Table i.1 provides a summary of the regions in this book and the countries included in these regions.

What Is Global?

The next issue that needs to be dealt with at the outset of this book is the completeness of its coverage. While the word *global* is used throughout the book, it is not actually global. It is based on 74 of the 240 countries listed in the United Nations website. The 74 included countries are important in that they account for 79 percent of the world's population as estimated by the UN and 92 percent of the global GDP as estimated by the International Monetary Fund. The gaps tend to be smaller countries (such as the Pacific Islands) for which there are good data available but the size is not significant, or countries for which reliable data are not available. Overall, the missing countries are on the margin; what happens to them will be less impactful on the world than what happens in many of the countries and regions covered in this book. For example, the regions in this book of North America, Western Europe, and Affluent Asia may only account for 15 percent of the world's population but they account for 65 percent of the total earned income in the world. So changes in expenditure patterns in these three regions will have a very significant impact on the opportunities for business. Such could not be said for, say, the Pacific Islands as a group.

The biggest gap in terms of coverage is, however, sub-Saharan Africa. Generally speaking, the data available for this region are very poor with respect to completeness, reliability, and time series. For three

Table i.1 Regions, the Countries in Them and Value on Key Dimensions 2012

Region	Country	Population 000s	Rank	Total GDP US$ Bns	Rank	Consumer Market Value US$ Bns	Rank	Consumption per Capita US$	Rank
Central and South America									
	Argentina	40,909	26	418	26	239	24	5,840	43
	Brazil	195,478	5	2,214	7	1,332	7	6,813	40
	Chile	17,474	40	227	41	130	43	7,432	37
	Colombia	46,581	23	316	33	198	30	4,248	48
	Mexico	112,565	10	1,112	14	731	13	6,496	41
	Puerto Rico	4,030	65	101	56	60	56	14,790	26
	Peru	29,115	33	176	47	107	45	3,679	50
	Venezuela	30,277	31	417	27	237	25	7,821	35
Western Europe									
	Austria	8,441	52	398	29	216	26	25,626	11
	Belgium	10,523	47	488	22	256	22	24,353	13
	Denmark	5,554	57	319	31	156	36	28,169	6
	Finland	5,321	59	253	36	138	40	25,922	10
	France	64,426	19	2,606	5	1,519	5	23,570	15
	Germany	81,587	14	3,389	4	1,947	4	23,865	14
	Greece	11,295	44	280	34	210	27	18,555	22
	Iceland	331	73	13	68	7	72	20,430	19
	Ireland	4,597	62	240	39	123	44	26,700	8
	Italy	60,510	21	2,014	8	1,216	8	20,104	20
	Netherlands	16,665	41	802	16	363	18	21,800	17

(Continued)

Table i.1 *(Continued)*

Region	Country	Population		Total GDP		Consumer Market Value		Consumption per Capita	
		000s	Rank	US$ Bns	Rank	US$ Bns	Rank	US$	Rank
	Norway	4,874	61	431	25	185	32	37,881	2
	Portugal	10,556	46	220	43	147	39	13,894	28
	Spain	46,235	24	1,393	12	813	12	17,589	23
	Sweden	9,391	50	497	21	240	23	25,597	12
	Switzerland	7,822	54	547	19	318	19	40,631	1
	United Kingdom	63,881	20	2,287	6	1,473	6	23,060	16
Eastern Europe									
	Armenia	3,338	69	10	72	7	71	2,193	57
	Albania	3,341	68	13	71	11	67	3,236	52
	Azerbaijan	9,004	51	56	60	24	64	2,653	55
	Belarus	9,420	49	58	58	32	59	3,424	51
	Bulgaria	7,306	55	50	61	30	60	4,058	49
	Czech Republic	10,575	45	205	45	103	47	9,767	31
	Estonia	1,348	71	21	67	11	66	8,072	33
	Georgia	4,466	63	13	69	10	68	2,193	56
	Hungary	9,923	48	133	53	71	54	7,149	39
	Kazakhstan	16,613	42	165	50	74	53	4,461	46
	Latvia	2,205	70	26	66	16	65	7,158	38
	Lithuania	3,348	67	40	62	26	62	7,849	34
	Moldova	3,599	66	6	73	6	73	1,561	66
	Poland	37,845	27	502	20	307	20	8,108	32

Romania	21,335	38	170	49	106	46	4,964	45
Russia	141,626	8	1,591	11	825	11	5,824	44
Turkey	74,961	17	800	18	569	16	7,595	36
Ukraine	44,905	25	151	51	97	48	2,150	58

North Africa and Middle East

Algeria	36,173	28	172	48	62	55	1,703	64
Egypt	79,366	15	222	42	166	33	2,088	59
Iran	76,763	16	410	28	208	28	2,714	54
Israel	8,089	53	236	40	138	41	17,011	25
Morocco	33,247	30	100	57	58	57	1,736	63
Saudi Arabia	26,648	34	480	23	163	34	6,112	42
UAE	5,358	58	319	32	200	29	37,343	3
Ethiopia	89,834	12	31	65	26	63	292	73
Yemen	24,527	35	36	63	29	61	1,188	67

North America

United States	316,266	3	14,972	1	10,622	1	33,585	4
Canada	34,771	29	1,641	10	940	10	27,033	7

Affluent Asia

Australia	22,437	37	1,338	13	706	14	31,445	5
Hong Kong	7,115	56	248	37	154	37	21,693	18
Japan	127,368	9	5,502	3	3,349	2	26,290	9
Korea	48,172	22	1,100	15	578	15	12,004	29
Macau	580	72	31	64	8	70	14,326	27
New Zealand	4,441	64	150	52	87	50	19,607	21

(Continued)

Table i.1 (Continued)

Region	Country	Population		Total GDP		Consumer Market Value		Consumption per Capita	
		000s	Rank	US$ Bns	Rank	US$ Bns	Rank	US$	Rank
	Singapore	5,305	60	245	38	93	49	17,462	24
	Taiwan	23,145	36	451	24	262	21	11,309	30
Developing Asia									
	Bangladesh	156,244	7	112	55	85	51	541	72
	Cambodia	14,319	43	13	70	10	69	669	71
	Indonesia	236,453	4	800	17	454	17	1,919	60
	Malaysia	29,532	32	263	35	131	42	4,444	47
	Pakistan	166,667	6	185	46	153	38	919	69
	Philippines	97,986	11	219	44	157	35	1,602	65
	Sri Lanka	21,121	39	56	59	37	58	1,749	62
	Thailand	67,031	18	346	30	190	31	2,841	53
	Vietnam	86,731	13	117	54	78	52	901	70
India		1,192,419	2	1,979	9	1,132	9	949	68
China		1,347,602	1	7,446	2	2,493	3	1,850	61

of the larger countries in that region, specifically South Africa, Kenya and Nigeria, data are available, but they account in total for a small proportion of the estimated total population of the sub-Saharan region and are probably not representative. So, that region is missing from this analysis. Owing to its relatively high poverty, it is not important economically (although many regard it as a growth opportunity), although clearly it is as important as South America in terms of population. But, with the lack of reliable data (many countries in this region do not have a functioning census and statistics department), little reliable estimation can be done in respect of it. For that reason, it is excluded from this analysis of the future demography of the world.

Reliability

The value of this book is that it provides the reader with a view of how the world might be expected to change over the next 20 years in terms of population, households, labour force, household incomes, and expenditure patterns. Clearly there has to be a basis for these forecasts. The underlying data are that released by the census and statistics department/ national bureau of statistics or equivalent for each of the countries covered. This information is supplemented with data from UN, IMF, WHO, ILO and the World Bank, basically to check from as many dimensions as possible whether the source data are consistent. The data are then checked in terms of relationships and trends to ensure that it meets certain normative behaviour. Once the data have been checked for completeness and consistency of behaviour, they are modeled using econometric style models, often with constraints in terms of how different variables fit together.

Clearly, the reliability of the source data does vary by country. Some are very precise and timely; for others, the data vary significantly year by year, are late being published and are not always complete. Our own models are used to try to deal with these issues and give (as a result of having a times series as well as comparative data from other countries) a better understanding of the exact values of the historic data, or at least the range it would fall within.

As soon as the data have been cleaned and the relationships within it modeled (e.g., the trend in household size is a function of the trend in the age distribution of the population) the statistical relationships (equations) are then used to forecast forward 40 years; although, of course, that is too far to be reliable, it is a useful way to ensure the long-term trend is sensible. It is these forecasts that are the raw material for this book.

The forecasts are considered reliable subject to the following:

1. They are based on trends in key variables (such as birth rates by age of mother) and the pattern of interrelationships (for example, the relationship between affluence and the propensity to have children) of the last two decades. For most of the key demographic variables such as birth rates and death rates, household size, propensity to be employed, propensity to be enrolled in school and so on, the trend over time tends to be quite consistent. The data points will vary year on year around the trend line, but overall they vary little from the trend over a 5- or 10-year period. This means that for the majority of countries, particularly those which have proportionately low levels of immigration, the forecast profile of the population, households, and labour force tends to be quite reliable, especially for the next 20 years, as much of the population that will affect these variables (e.g., the number of women who will have children) are already alive today.

2. However, some aspects of demographics can be disrupted, typically by government action which cannot be forecast with any degree of reliability. Fortunately, from a forecasting point of view, the propensity of governments to make draconian decision similar to that of China's one-child policy is low. But they do make decisions in terms of migration levels, and at the time of writing (2012) many governments are revisiting this issue, generally with a view to limiting the level below that of the past decade. This cannot be forecast and the models assume that the levels of migration in the future will follow the age, gender profile and average quantity of the last five years, taking into account average income differentials between countries (migrants follow money: few people move to a country that is less affluent than their current country). For most countries immigration is not significant as a proportion of total population nor in terms of impact on the future profile of the population (although generally immigrants lower the age profile slightly and increase births), but

for countries such as Singapore, Australia, New Zealand, the United States, Canada, and some of the more prosperous Western European countries, it would mean the forecasts would be different from actual in 20 years if immigration level is reduced significantly from its current levels. Basically, if immigration was constrained below current levels, these populations would grow significantly more slowly than that currently forecast and the age bias would be older.

3. The other area that is less reliable in terms of forecast is household incomes and, by implication, expenditure levels. For reasons explained in detail later (although it is intuitively obvious), average and median household incomes are directly a function of GDP (and, more specifically, the Private Consumption Expenditure Component [PCE] of GDP) and forecasting total real GDP in 20 years is, of course, problematic. It is difficult to get it right for next year! So, it has to be accepted that forecasts in terms of household income and expenditure are less reliable and could vary substantially from that shown. We do, of course, try to minimise the random nature of these forecasts. There are certain basic components to GDP and the proportion of it that reaches the consumer, and these tend to have a degree of consistency to them. Collectively, they determine certain minimums in terms of what GDP can be.

To explain, in its simplest form, total GDP is a function of the following inputs: The first is the size of the workforce. This is determined by the number of persons of working age and their propensity to be employed. The number of persons of working age is itself a function of the age profile of the population, which, as stated earlier, can be forecast with relatively high reliability. Propensity to be employed can vary, but historical evidence shows quite firmly that over a five-year period it is very consistent in its pattern and trend. So the future size of the workforce can be predicted with some confidence.

The second key input is the gross productivity of this workforce. That is the total GDP divided by the number of workers. On a per country basis, this has quite a consistent relationship with the trend in the education profile of the adult population. As education improves so the productivity of the worker lifts in a consistent pattern. As the education profile of an adult population of a country does not change dramatically year by year (it is a function of the changing education profile of the relatively small proportion of the population that enter and leave the working age range year by year), this means the core productive capability of the workforce also moves in a steady direction. By multiplying these two variables—the number of employed persons and the productivity per worker—we get a base-line estimate of what the total GDP can be expected to be.

On a historical basis, this approach has been a good indicator for economies that are considered more mature in nature. It does, however, underestimate the future GDP values for economies that are going through some form of structural change such as sudden increases in unemployment in Spain, Greece, and France in the current (2012) economic crisis as a result of the government needing to realign its public spending with the earning capacity of the overall economy, and the rapid increase in fixed capital investment that took place in China; over the last ten years 40 percent of the total GDP growth in China was fixed capital investment. In both these cases market forces will ultimately bring them back to normative behaviour and as such, the 20-year forecast based on size of labour force and productivity as a function of education trends tend to be good base-line indicators. So treat that aspect of this book as the conservative or worst-case scenarios for trends in household incomes and expenditure trends.

Sources

The databases used for the analysis reported in this book are quite extensive, covering 74 countries, as well as regions within China and India. The databases are really made up of three parts. There is the source data, which are the historical values on the relevant variables as reported by the appropriate organisations. The data are then harmonised and cleaned to remove inconsistencies and illogical values. Finally, the cleaned historical data are modelled mathematically, and those equations are then used in an econometric style model to provide forecast of each of the variables. So the forecasts, and much of the historical data, are effectively generated by Global Demographics models, and that is the source for the information provided in this book.

However, the original data are from a variety of sources, which will be summarised here. The primary source is the state statistical bureau, national statistics office, or census office of each country. (The name of the organisation does vary across countries but is essentially the government office responsible for collecting basic population and economic statistics on the country.) Global Demographics also obtains the data as reported to the United Nations, International Monetary Fund, The World Bank, The World Health Organisation, and The International Labour Organisation, as these provide a cross check on the published data and also a degree of harmonisation on certain aspects of it. Finally, data are obtained where possible from other government departments such as Ministry of Education. These multiple sources help to check that data are within a reasonable range and that they make sense in a holistic sense. For example, it is reasonable to expect that in a country where education is compulsory and free for 6- to 12-year-olds that the total enrollment for that age range as reported by the Department of Education are not out of line with the total number of births that took place between 6 and 12 years ago.

Getting Value from This Book

The value of the information contained in this book is not so much the forecasts provided—although, of course, they should add to your overall knowledge—but rather, what you do with this information. If it helps you test the veracity of current perceptions about how the world is developing, then it has served a useful role—irrespective of whether it confirms or refutes your current perceptions. At least you have challenged your normative view and reached an opinion about its voracity or modified it accordingly.

The second potential contribution of this book is that it provides you with a framework in which to evaluate specific countries or markets. To that end, Figure i.1 is the first step in that direction, as it provides a good visual summary of how the regions compare to each other. There are three dimensions to Figure i.1. The first is the horizontal axis—the further a country or region is to the right the greater is the proportion of its population that is over 40 years of age (which is a significant age point

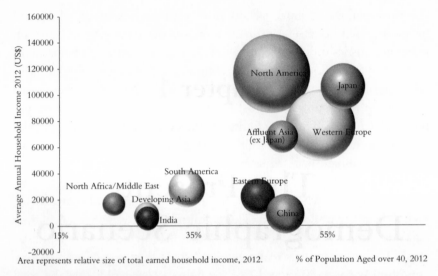

Area represents relative size of total earned household income, 2012.   % of Population Aged over 40, 2012

Figure i.1 The Relative Positions and Importance of Individual Regions in 2012

Source: Global Demographics Ltd.

as that is where changes start to take place in household consumption patterns). The vertical axis is the average household income of all households in the country or region and demonstrates their individual relative affluence and is a good proxy for the price points at which they spend and level of education. Finally, the size of the circles is the relative share of total earned income in the world (or rather the 74 countries covered in this book) accounted for by each region/country.

As the reader will see, there are effectively three main groupings of regions (and countries). There are the old affluent, the young poor, and finally the old poor. Each of these positions significantly determines how those regions will develop over the next 20 years—and this starting point and its relevance to the future is the subject of Chapter 1.

Chapter 1

The Present
Demographic Scenario

D emography fundamentally shapes our social and economic
environment and almost every aspect of our lives. Dealing
with life, death, ageing, education, households, consumption,
development, the environment, progress, wealth, opportunity and
many other vital and compelling issues, its significance cannot be
overstated. Yet despite its importance for the future of individuals,
businesses, governments, and entire societies, it is a subject that is often
misunderstood or simply ignored. It is important to understand how
demography is changing and where we are heading. If we are to avoid a
directionless, haphazard road, we need to take control and prepare for
the future, and this begins by having a better understanding of what
demography is telling us about the future.

This book follows humanity's journey into the future. As with all
journeys it pays to know where we are starting, and this is especially true

when it comes to demographic and socioeconomic forecasting. After all, the population profile that exists today will largely determine the population and socioeconomic profile existing in 20 years. With demography, there is a high degree of certainty in the forecasts that are made and the changes identified will encompass issues ranging from changing population age profiles, the new household structure, changing labour force profiles and incomes and expenditure patterns.

> *The population profile that exists today will significantly influence the population and socio-economic profile existing in 20 years.*

In this chapter, we highlight the most significant facts about populations and demography, and subsequent chapters explain the implications and trajectory resulting from the current demographic scenario. Simply put, we need to know where we are now if we are to understand where we are heading. Knowing how demography will unfold over the next 20 years and appreciating the implications of these developments matters for many reasons. As well as being useful for individuals to understand, the demographic developments are also vitally important for policy makers in government and decision makers in business.

So, what is the truth about the global population today, and what are the implications for the future?

The Current State of Global Demography

A useful way of looking at the world[1] is shown in Figure 1.1, the Age and Affluence Profile. This chart displays the three dimensions that

---

The reader is reminded again that the words *global* and *world* in the context of this book are used to apply to the 74 countries included in the analysis. These account for an estimated 79% of the total population on the planet and 92% of its estimated GDP. The gap is mainly sub-Saharan Africa on which there is not sufficient data available for forecasting purposes.

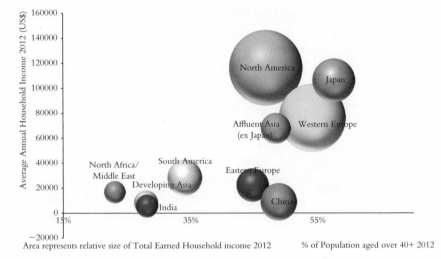

Figure 1.1 The Age and Affluence Profile of the World 2012
Source: Global Demographics Ltd.

are driving demographic change. First, the vertical axis is estimated average household income in US$ in 2012, which is a good indication of the relative purchasing power of the community, education levels (education and income are highly correlated) and productive capacity. Second, the horizontal axis is the percentage of the population that is aged over 40 years, which has implications for family age structure, household size and future growth rates of the population, as well as current patterns of consumption. Finally, the size of each ball corresponds to the aggregate spending power of the region, derived by multiplying the average household income by the number of households in the region and shows the relative importance of each from a consumption power perspective.

The first point to note is that the world in 2012 can be divided into three main groups. At the top right of Figure 1.1 is the first group: the old and affluent. Accounting for 18 percent of global population and 71 percent of income, these countries are the very important consumers and economies of today. These affluent regions include: North America; all of Western Europe; Japan and Affluent Asia, consisting of South

Table 1.1　Share of Global Household Income Growth

	Share of Global Income Growth	
	2002–12	2012–32
North America	22%	23%
Western Europe	11%	6%
Affluent Asia	12%	14%
South America	9%	9%
Eastern Europe	10%	5%
North Africa Middle East	4%	3%
China	21%	25%
Developing Asia	5%	6%
India	6%	8%

SOURCE: Global Demographics Ltd.

Korea, Taiwan, Singapore, Hong Kong, Australia, and New Zealand. In nearly all of these countries:

- Close to 50 percent or more of the population are over the age of 40.
- The childless household is increasingly the norm, as is the one or two-adult household.
- Households typically have an income in excess of US$50,000 per annum.

It should also be recognised at this point that, while they might have slower growth rates than other economies, they are nonetheless growing and, as shown in Table 1.1, in absolute terms, have accounted for 45 percent of the increase in consumer incomes on a global basis over the last decade even though they are just 18 percent of the population.

In contrast, the second grouping rests at the bottom left of Figure 1.1 and is home to the young and the poor—countries that have a young age-profile and are relatively poor. Many countries in these regions have nearly one third of their population under the age of 15 and, in some cases, over 50 percent of the population is under the age of 25 years. Average household income is US$20,000 or less and 70 percent are in households with an annual income below US$10,000. Countries in these regions face a problem in that many of the households have multiple dependents for each wage earner, which limits their ability to educate their children and save—a problem compounded by the low wage. Looking again at the size of each ball for such regions, it is apparent that they are less significant in terms of total consumption power. Despite frequently voiced views to the contrary, in total, India, the Middle East, North Africa, and Developing Asia account for no more than 9 percent of all household income in the world, but contain 43 percent of the population in the regions covered by this book.

The third group consists of Eastern Europe and China and is different from the other two groups by being both relatively poor and old. The incomes in these regions are higher than those in the lower left group but remain substantially below those of the affluent region. Average annual before tax household income in Eastern Europe is US$22,670 while in China it is US$9,500. What distinguishes them from the countries on the left of Figure 1.1 is that they are significantly older (over 45 percent of their populations are over 40 years of age), which means that they have a smaller average household size (children have typically grown up and left home or are economically independent and consequently 55 percent of the households are childless even in 2012), giving them a greater ability to engage in discretionary expenditure and to save in spite of their low incomes.

While grouping countries by region often makes sense, the reader should appreciate that there are inevitably outliers—that is, exceptions that should be kept in mind. For example, Middle East and North Africa, which have an average household income of US$17,000, include some countries where the average household income is in excess of US$50,000. Despite this, a regional perspective rather than a national one is more useful to our understanding of the journey into the future. Otherwise the reader will be lost in myriad statistics and lose sight of key themes. By breaking down the population into regions, we can see how developments by region affect the way that the world develops as a whole. India and China account for such a significant proportion of the world's population that what happens there echoes on the world stage, and for this reason they are treated as regions in their own right. Analysis of the regions does confirm (albeit contrary to the above point) the countries within a specific region typically have more in common with each other than with countries in other regions.

Where Is Everyone?

To examine the existing demographic and socioeconomic profile of the world it is useful to start by looking at the share of the world's population accounted for by each region.

Figure 1.2 shows the estimated number (in millions of people) and proportion of the world's population in 2012 that is currently located in each region. India and China account for 21 percent and 24 percent, respectively, of the total population covered in the 74 countries included in the study. Nearly one out of every two people lives in either China or India. If we then broaden this to Developing Asia—which includes Indonesia, Pakistan, Malaysia, Bangladesh, Thailand, the Philippines, and Vietnam—then this Asian region accounts for 61 percent of the global population (or nearly two out of every three people). South America is a further 8 percent, Middle East and North Africa 7 percent, Eastern Europe 7 percent, leaving 18 percent for the old (in terms of population age profile) countries of the world—North America, Western Europe, and Affluent Asia.

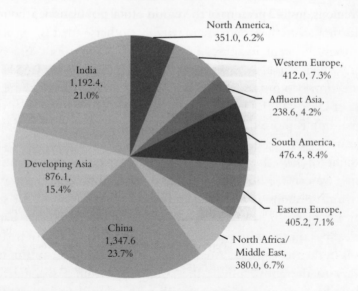

Figure 1.2 Population of Regions Covered (2012)
Source: Global Demographics Ltd.

Age Profile

It is important to appreciate that today's age profile has significant implications for what the population of countries will be like in the future. For example, the number of females under the age of 20 significantly determines the number of births that will take place in 20 years, as they will effectively determine the number of women of childbearing age in 2032. So we have a number of good and very reliable indicators of how some aspects of each society will change simply by looking at the existing age profile.

As we've already seen, the world divides between those countries whose population is biased towards persons under the age of 25 and those biased to those over the age of 40. South America is in the midpoint between these two groups. To give an example of the extremes, Figure 1.3 profiles the regional age profile.

Looking at the younger regions first, specifically Developing Asia, India and Africa, just on 31 percent of their existing population are under the age of 15 and a further 18 percent are under the age of 24. These countries have a youth population of 747 million people aged 0 to 14 years of age and a further 457 million aged 15 to 24 years of age. These three regions, just 42 percent of the world's total population, account for

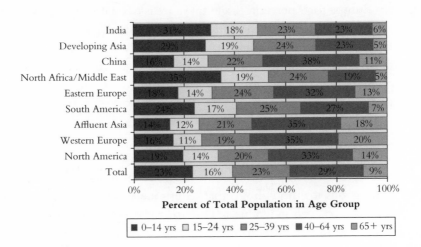

Figure 1.3 Age Profile by Region (2012)
Source: Global Demographics Ltd.

54 percent of all people in the world under the age of 25 years. If South America is added to this, then 58 percent of all young people are found in these regions.

It is important to understand the implications of youth for a country. The young populations of the world are both a significant determinant of the size and education profile of the labour force in 20 years, as well as the number of future consumers. However, young people are also a significant economic drain on the economy. They have no inherent savings on which to draw, but require education and health care, as well as the basics of clothing, food, and housing. While they represent a potential benefit to society in the future (an issue that is explored in the next chapter), the reality is that they are a significant liability at present.

Having briefly considered the issue of youth, it's time to look at the other end of the age dimension: those people over the age of 40. Clearly, this is an area where China dominates. It is estimated that, in 2012, 31 percent of all people in the world over the age of 40 are located in China. A further 23 percent are located in North America, Western Europe and Affluent Asia. To put that in context, it should be appreciated that those last three regions account for 18 percent of the world population. If the focus is moved to those over the age of 65 years, North America, Western Europe, and Affluent Asia account for a third of all such persons, while China accounts for a further 28 percent and Eastern Europe for 9 percent. Just as there are issues with having a young population, so there are with having an old population. Old people are less likely to be employed and have significantly higher demands on health care. With improving health care, life expectancy is increasing with implications for labour force size, recreation, pensions, and welfare demands in 20 years.

The Household

This brings us to the importance of the nature of the household. After all, for many goods it is households that determine what is consumed, not communities or even individuals. The structure and number of households are both important variables. In 2012, there were estimated to be 1.6 billion households in the 74 countries covered by this analysis, giving an average household size of around 3.5 persons. However, as shown in

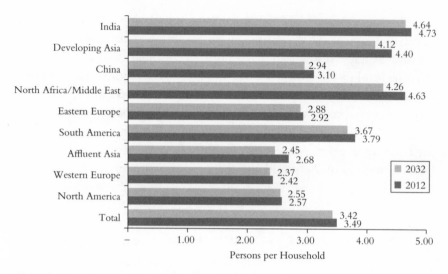

Figure 1.4 Average Household Size (2012)
Source: Global Demographics Ltd.

Figure 1.4, there are significant differences in average household size between regions; for instance, in the older regions of North America, Western Europe, and Affluent Asia, the average household size is 2.4 to 2.7 persons.

This is different from what we see in the younger countries, where the average household size is 4.4 people or more. This difference is a function of household composition. It is safe to generalise that in the older regions, the smaller household consists of one or two adults and, at most, one child. As a result, the number of dependents per wage earner in these households is quite low, with an average of around 1.1 people dependent on each wage earner (many households in these regions have no dependent children).

In the younger regions, the typical household consists of two adults and two or more children and, because these countries also have lower labour force participation rates amongst adults, the number of dependents per wage earner is typically greater than 1.4, which has a significant implication on funds available for each individual (that is, on a per capita basis).

In this respect, it is interesting to compare India and China. Relatively similar household incomes produce very different per capita household incomes. In India, a household earning (say) US$3000 per annum has a *per capita* income of US$634, as average household size at that income level in India is 4.7. In China, with its much older population and smaller average household size, both in absolute terms and at that income level (3.1 persons), a US$3000 household income translates into US$967 per capita. This is approximately 50 percent more than the income per capita in an Indian household with the same total income. Obviously, this has an enormous impact on the type of consumption that can take place. This same dichotomy exists between the older, affluent regions of the world and the young, poor regions of the world.

Urbanisation

After age and income, we come to the next force affecting our present and shaping our future: urbanisation. In the more affluent countries, population is already significantly urban. North America, Western Europe, and Affluent Asia have over 80 percent of their populations living in urban areas. Rural populations are a significantly higher proportion of the total population (two out of every three people) in Developing Asia, India, and, to a lesser extent, the Middle East and North Africa. In China, it is lower, at one person in two. This issue is significant, because people living in rural areas earn less, typically have larger families, and are not as well educated. As a result, rural populations tend to suffer the consequences of being young, badly educated, and poor. On average, a rural household will have an income percent of about half that of an urban household in the same country. At the same time, it will have at least one additional person to support at that lower income, with implications for per capita income.

On average, a rural household will have an income about half that of an urban household. At the same time, it will have at least one additional person, with implications for per capita income.

It is interesting to think through the implications of this issue for China. In 2012, the average urban household has an estimated income, before tax, of US$13,689, compared with US$4,336 for the average rural household. The per capita household income for urban households is US$5,370 whereas for a rural household it is US$1,201, or less than one-third that of an urban household, hence the motivation for rural–urban migration. In India the same motivation exists—but the differential is less.

Education

The next critical component of today's demographics is education. This is difficult to measure for several reasons, but chiefly because there are differences in the ages of entry to and exit from the education system, as well as a problem with definitions. For example, what precisely is meant by *secondary education*? The age range and number of years differ by country. Because of these challenges we have developed a single index that is based on the amount of time spent in the education system, rather than the specific categories, with an increasing weight placed on increasing number of years; that is, a higher qualification such as a diploma is worth significantly more than a lower one—completed primary—in terms of potential productivity. Figure 1.5 plots the position of the different countries on this index in 2012 and shows this

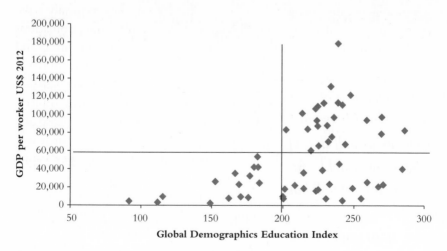

Figure 1.5 A Global View of Education and Productivity (2012)
Source: Global Demographics Ltd.

against GDP per employed persons—a reasonably stable measure of productivity.

While the relationship is statistically weak across countries, it is quite strong within each country over time, showing good correlation between overall education standard of adults and productivity per worker. However, the cross-country comparison does nonetheless appear to demonstrate the common sense conclusion that education is a necessary, but not sufficient, condition to accelerate productivity per worker. Below an index value of 200, where the majority of the population has only completed primary education, there are no countries with a GDP per worker in excess of US$65,000 per annum. Above that point a country is as likely to have higher productivity per worker as to not have it—the difference being probably a function of labour laws, cultural attitudes to work, working hours, and so on.

The essential issue here is that after reaching 200 on the index there is potentially a very significant payoff—suggesting a tipping point at which, under the right environment, capital investment flows to the worker and rapidly lifts their productivity. Unfortunately, at present (2012), an estimated 73 percent of the total workforce in the regions covered by this book are living in countries with an education index at or below 200.

Lifting the standard of education is (or should be) a priority of any government. But it must be recognised that this is not something that happens overnight. Improving education standards today will take a good 10 to 20 years to impact the skill set of the workforce. However, one happy irony of this is that the countries with the lowest education profiles today have youthful populations, which means that the extent to which the education profile of the future labour force will change over time is high. For example, in India, between now and 2032 as much as 49 percent of the people in the labour force in 2032 will have joined it after 2012. So, improvements in the education system *now* will have a significant impact on the potential skill set of the labour force in 20 years in these young countries. By comparison, China with its much older (and better educated) population, the equivalent proportion of its 2032 labour force that will enter between 2012 and 2032 is just 31 percent. This means a slower future lift in the education profile of China's labour force.

Apart from demonstrating how much of today's demographic profile will impact the future productive capability of individual countries and regions, it also stresses how important it is that these young countries act now. Improved education impacts not only the earning ability of the labour force but also fertility, nutrition, health care, and life expectancy. Education is one of the most critical variables to monitor when assessing the future outlook

49 percent of India's labour force in 2032 will have joined it between 2012 and 2032—this gives that young country a chance to upskill more rapidly than older countries.

of a country or region. Money spent on education rather than space programs will produce a greater benefit for society.

Employment

The next issue to consider is employment. Employment is a function of two factors. First, the propensity of a person of working age to be employed and second, the number of persons who are of working age. Propensity to be employed is defined as the proportion of people of working age that are working and contributing to the total economy of the country. Globally, this varies in several important ways. First, there are significant regional differences in the propensity of females to be employed. Second, there is an increasing difference between regions in what is defined as working age. Because of this, it is useful to begin this journey into the future with an understanding of the current scenarios.

Table 1.2 shows the capacity in each society's economic engine given its 2012 norms. There is surprising little difference among regions/countries in terms of the proportion of the population that is of working age (defined as 15 to 64 years in 2012). The average for all is 67 percent, which means overall two out of three people in the regions covered are potential workers. As discussed later in this book, the concept of working age is changing—lengthening to age 69 and beyond—in some regions, and this will impact the extent to which the core resource of the economy contracts or expands over the next decade. But for now

Table 1.2   Percentage of Each Gender That Is Employed (2012)

2012	% of Population That Is Working Age	% of Working Age That Is Employed	
		Males	Females
Total	67%	77%	54%
North America	71%	73%	63%
Western Europe	70%	70%	57%
Affluent Asia	67%	78%	58%
South America	69%	73%	49%
Eastern Europe	70%	67%	55%
North Africa/Middle East	61%	76%	30%
China	73%	83%	71%
Developing Asia	66%	82%	44%
India	64%	75%	39%

SOURCE: Global Demographics Ltd.
NOTE: Working age is defined as 15 to 69 years for North America, Western Europe, and Affluent Asia. It is 15 to 64 for all other regions.

two-thirds of the population are in the working age band. Younger countries and regions, such as North Africa and the Middle East, have a lower proportion for now as so many of their populations are under 15 years of age, but this changes (increases) significantly over the next two decades, as shown later in this book.

The next two columns are the propensity of the working-age population to be employed by gender, as there are significant differences. In this regard, female participation rates are particularly important. Female participation ranges from a low of 30 percent in the Middle East and North Africa to a high of 71 percent in China. This has a significant implication for the size of the labour force, as well as the ratio of dependents per employed person, which in turn impacts the income per capita in the household and capability of the household to consume or save. For China, with 71 percent of females and 83 percent of males of working age in employment (effectively running at full capacity), the number of dependents per worker is quite low at less than 1 dependent for every working person. Similarly, in affluent countries, where typically two-thirds of females and three-quarters of males of working age are employed, the dependency ratio is low at just over 1 dependent per worker. This contrasts with Developing Asia, South America, India, North Africa, and the Middle East, where the proportion of females of working age that is employed is less than 50 percent, with consequent implications for the existing dependency ratio, which ranges between 1.4 and 2.0 dependents supported by every worker. That means in these regions a worker is supporting around 2.4 to 3.0 persons—themselves and 1.4 to 2.0 others.

The participation rates and, particularly, the differences in female participation rates, are important, as much is made about unemployment statistics (e.g., 20 percent of youth who are seeking work in Spain are unemployed), but the reality is that productive power is a function of the proportion of total population employed and not the proportion of the population seeking work that is not employed (the standard definition of unemployment). For example, in Spain, 46 percent of its population is employed (as female participation is quite high). This compares with, say, India, where only 37 percent of its population is employed, as a result of very low female participation rates.

Participation rates combined with changes in population age profile and working age definition have direct implications for the subsequent size of the labour force and growth of the economy. While this chapter is about now, it is useful here to take a peek into the future in this respect.

In China, its existing high female (and male) participation rates mean that it has absolutely no spare labour capacity and, consequently, given its total population as well as working age population is now flat or declining, it means that its total labour force will also inevitably decline. With that, the growth of its economy will become increasingly a function of its ability to lift productivity per worker, primarily through education. Compare that with India, where working-age population increases in absolute terms for the next two

By changing the education profile of its females and acceptance of women in the workforce, India's labour force could quickly expand from being only 58 percent that of China's to being far greater.

decades. By changing the education profile of its females and the acceptance of women in the workforce, India's labour force could quickly expand from being only 58 percent of China's to being far greater. This is examined in more detail in Chapter 5.

Household Income

The final, critical part of our understanding of where we are in 2012 is provided by household income. As household income determines consumption, it is useful to understand current income levels before considering how they might develop in the future. The first thing to note is the quite dramatic differences among regions, highlighted by Figure 1.6.

The figures in this chart have been determined using the average exchange rate of the local currency to US$ for the whole of 2011.

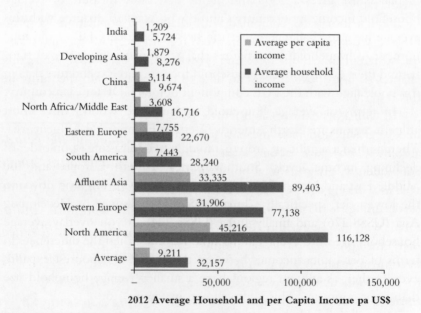

Figure 1.6 2012 Average Household and Annual per Capita Income US$
Source: Global Demographics Ltd.

Obviously exchange rates do vary even over the short term, and this will impact on the numbers shown here.

At this moment it is important to digress slightly and explain the reliability of the figures given. Generally people like to disagree with reported average household incomes—quoting the undeclared economy and thereby being able to make (often silly) claims about how much higher incomes are in a country. However, there is a very reliable indicator of average incomes. That is the household consumption expenditure, which is a part of private consumption expenditure (PCE), which in turn is a component of GDP. This is determined from expenditure data (e.g., retail sales) and thereby picks up the entire expenditure side of the households, irrespective of whether or not the income behind that expenditure has been declared for tax or survey purposes. As such, total household private consumption expenditure of GDP divided by the total households gives a clean measure of average household expenditure. This resulting figure, adjusted for propensity to spend and tax rates (good indicators of which can be obtained from household income and expenditure surveys done by most countries on a regular basis), gives a good and highly defensible measure of average household income in a country. Those who want to disagree with this average have to challenge either the size of the total GDP or the total number of households, two figures that tend to have a degree of rigor behind their estimation. All Household Income and Expenditure data in this book align with the PCE component of total GDP for each country.

In terms of average household income, the world's three most affluent regions are North America, Western Europe, and Affluent Asia. There is then a significant drop to a middle tier consisting of (in order of declining income levels) South America, Eastern Europe, and the Middle East and North Africa. There then follows a big drop down to the lowest tier, specifically China (US$9,674) followed by Developing Asia (US$8,276) and finally India (US$5,724). If you overlay average household size onto average household incomes, then the differences in terms of per capita incomes between the richest and poorest expands even further, as affluent regions have a smaller average household size than poor countries. This is also shown in Figure 1.6.

As well as highlighting differences in terms of average household incomes, it is useful in this review of where we are now to look at the

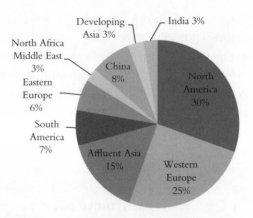

Figure 1.7 Global Shares of Total Household Incomes 2012
Source: Global Demographics Ltd.

distribution of *total* purchasing power—in other words, the sum of household incomes by region, which is average household income of each country in the region multiplied by the number of households in the country, summed for all countries in the region. The difference in income levels is such that the regions with smaller populations but significantly higher incomes account for a very substantial proportion of the total earned incomes worldwide, as shown in Figure 1.7. The world's three most affluent regions, specifically North America, Affluent Asia, and Western Europe, account for 18 percent of the population of the countries covered in this book, but a very significant 71 percent of the total world's earned incomes. The economies in these three regions are very important to the world's economic future and will remain so for some considerable time to come. In contrast, China and India combined, two countries with very large but relatively poor populations, account in total for just 11 percent of the world's total earned incomes. This fact is seriously at odds with the publicity given to the consumer markets in those countries. In some

The world's three most affluent regions account for 18 percent of the population of the countries covered in this book, but 71 percent of the total earned incomes.

cases this is because various parties multiply the total consumer expenditure by purchasing power parity index value. As explained later, purchasing power parity adjusts for the amount of goods and services that people in countries with a higher purchasing power can buy (at a cheaper and lower profit margin price), not the amount of money they have, so do not be fooled by those who multiply incomes by purchasing power parity, as it gives misleading impressions of the importance of some markets.

Summary

In this chapter, we have introduced the reader to the current state of those aspects of the demographics and socioeconomic profile of the world that we consider will be most influential in determining the future shape of global demography and socioeconomics.

It is significant that at present there is a wide disparity in terms of age, education, and affluence among regions. In particular, the countries with a bias to younger populations are typically poor and those countries with older (over 40 years) populations are typically rich. Effectively, this means that these two groups of countries/regions are moving into the future from two very different starting points and different levels of capability. Furthermore these starting points place constraints on the options open to them in terms of future development. For example, with its very large number of young females about to enter marrying age, it is going to be difficult for India to reduce its total births per annum, which in turn constrains its ability to provide education to all. Without lifting education the country cannot lift productivity of its workers and hence affluence.

These very different starting points for the world's regions and their populations are leading to very different outcomes in 20 years. This simple truth is one that is often overlooked. This is what this book will now examine, and in the coming chapters we explore the forces that are changing populations—including education, productivity, female participation in the workforce, income, and healthcare—as well as explaining the significance of these changes. We start in the next chapter by looking at population growth and the changing age profile of global population.

Chapter 2

Population Change
by 2032

This chapter explains how the world's population will change over the next 20 years given its existing age profile, trends in the propensity to have children, and death rates by age and gender. Specifically, we will see how the world's age profile is shifting, which, in turn, gives an indication of the likely nature of society and the products and services that will be required in the future.

In 2012, the total estimated population of the 74 countries included in this study was 5.67 billion people. As the United Nations estimates that there are 7.2 billion people alive at this time; this study accounts for 79 percent of the world's population. For each of these 74 countries

The existing age profile of a country or region significantly impacts the nature of its future population and economic growth.

we have reliable data on the birth rate, by age of mother and the death rate, by gender and age. Since birth and death rates within age groups do not vary significantly from the medium term trend line, using them gives reliable estimates of what total population will be in 2032 in these 74 countries: 6.385 billion. This represents an annual average growth rate of 0.6 percent including migration from regions not covered in this study. This total compares with the United Nations' forecast for global population in 2032 of 8.658 billion and indicates that they expect the population in the other countries (mainly in sub-Saharan Africa) to grow at 4.3 percent per annum. These are amongst the poorest regions of the world—with life expectancies of 40 years or less, incredibly high infant mortality rates, and HIV infection rates close to 20 percent—but also with exceptionally high birth rates, so making any forecast is difficult and there has to be an element of error in this forecast of 4.3 percent and probably it is an overstatement.

For the countries for which good data are available, the good news is that population growth is slowing and, with that, the pressure on the world's resources. However, it is the total that is slowing for, even within the set of countries covered in this book, there are some whose population will still increase in total over the next 20 years. Unfortunately, they tend to be the regions less able to provide for these additional people.

Migration, Births, and Death Rates

To understand how the total population figures will change we need to start by looking at the components of change—which is births, deaths, and net migration—and how they are changing in each of the regions over the next 20 years.

Managing Migration

One potential source of error in the population growth forecasts for the 74 countries included in this book is migration, which is often subject to unpredictable political forces. Unfortunately, there is no way that these changes in government policy can be predicted reliably.

So, the forecasts assume that the migration profile (number by age by gender) and trend (growing or declining) evident in the last five years for each country will continue over the next two decades. It should be noted that, because migrants tend to be younger, this does impact the number of childbearing women in the countries to which they migrate and that, in turn, has a significant impact on population growth rates. This applies particularly to North America, Singapore, and Australia.

Women of Childbearing Age

Births form the growth side of the population equation and total births in a country or region are the result of two factors: the number of women of childbearing age, and the propensity of these women to have a child. We will examine the characteristics of each factor separately.

Starting with the number of women of childbearing age, it is necessary to appreciate that while the age range being considered is 15 to 49, what really makes a difference is the number of women aged 20 to 34, as currently they are much more likely to have children than women aged 35 or older. While there is a trend away from that in the more affluent and better-educated countries, it is a slow-moving trend.

Based on the ageing trend in the populations covered, Global Demographics Ltd. forecasts indicate that the number of women of childbearing age globally is expected to remain largely constant over the next 20 years. In 2012, there are estimated to be 1,462 million women aged 15 to 49, and by 2032 this will only increase marginally to 1,481 million. The number of women that are age 15 to 34, being the age range at which the probability of having a child is highest, is estimated to be 860 million now and this will decline marginally to 838 million by 2032, which is significant, as this age group accounts for the majority of all births. These forecasts are reliable as the majority of these women are already alive today. However, there are considerable

> *Globally, the number of women of childbearing age is expected to remain largely constant over the next 20 years at around 1.5 billion.*

differences between regions in terms of the trend in number of
women of childbearing age. In Western Europe, Affluent Asia,
Eastern Europe, and China the number of women of childbearing age
is expected to decline. This contrasts with the Middle East/North
Africa, Developing Asia, and India, regions which are expected to
experience growth in the number of women of childbearing age, as
shown in Table 2.1. Finally, it is worth noting that South America is
now at a stage where the number of such women is constant (and will
start to decline after 2030).

As we saw in the previous chapter, the trends in India and China are
especially significant because together these two countries account for
45 percent of the total population of the countries covered in this book.
In India, there are 306 million women of childbearing age (196 million
aged 15 to 34 years) and this is expected to reach 373 million (228
million aged 15 to 34) by 2032. This represents a 22 percent increase in
the childbearing population of India and, as with so much in demography this is almost inevitable, as the majority of women who will be
aged 15 to 49 in 2032 are alive today as children. Unless something
catastrophic happens, the increase in the number of women in this age
group will definitely materialise.

In contrast, the number of Chinese women of childbearing age is
currently estimated at 354 million (177 million aged 15 to 34 years).
Because the number of total births has been declining for some years
now, the number of women of childbearing age in 2032 is projected to
decline to 254 million (122 million aged 15 to 34 years). This is a
reduction of 28 percent. Clearly, this will have a significant impact on
the total number of births in China in future years. This scenario will not
change significantly even if the one-child policy was relaxed immedi-
ately, as it would take 15 years for it to affect the number of women of
childbearing age and the one-child policy already only applies to about
38 percent of households. (See Chapter 10.)

Propensity to Have Children

The second component impacting total births is the propensity of women
of childbearing age to have a child, which is normally measured by the
number of births per thousand women of childbearing age. This is

Table 2.1 Women Age 15 to 49 Years (Millions) 2012 to 2032

	Women (Millions) 15–34 years			Women (Millions) 35–49 years			Women (Millions) 15–49 years	
	2012	2032	CAGR 2012–32	2012	2032	CAGR 2012–32	2012	2032
North America	47	51	0.4%	35	39	0.6%	82	90
Western Europe	47	45	−0.2%	44	38	−0.8%	92	83
Affluent Asia	29	23	−1.2%	26	21	−1.1%	55	44
South America	80	75	−0.4%	52	60	0.7%	132	135
Eastern Europe	60	47	−1.2%	44	43	0.0%	104	90
North Africa/Middle East	66	86	1.4%	31	47	2.2%	96	134
China	177	122	−1.8%	177	132	−1.4%	354	255
Developing Asia	158	161	0.1%	81	117	1.8%	239	278
India	196	228	0.8%	111	145	1.4%	306	373
Total	861	838	−0.1%	601	644	0.3%	1,462	1,482

SOURCE: Global Demographics Ltd. (estimates)

generally around 40 in more affluent countries and around 70 in less affluent ones. In Western Europe, the present low rate of 44.6 births per thousand women is projected to increase slightly over the next 20 years. It will also increase marginally in North America and Affluent Asia. For every other region, the propensity to have a child is declining. There is a particularly rapid decline occurring in India, reflecting a significant change in attitudes, and this is expected to continue as a result of the country's steadily increasing affluence and improving educational standards. China, with one of the lowest birth rates in the world, is projected to continue with a small decline in average birth rate, as the population increasingly accepts the norm of one child and as the bias of women of childbearing age moves out of the 15 to 34 year age group and into the 35 to 49 age group, which has a significantly lower propensity to have children.

The projected changes in the number of births per thousand women of childbearing age between 2012 and 2032, given forecast trends in education and affluence and their impact on propensity to have a child for each region, is highlighted in Figure 2.1. It is

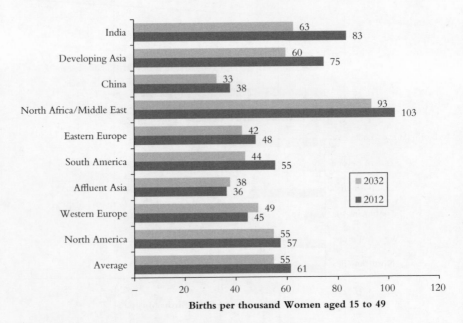

Figure 2.1 Births per Thousand Women Age 15 to 49
Source: Global Demographics Ltd.

increasing in Western Europe and Affluent Asia and declining in the rest. Fortunately it is declining in those regions in which the birth rate is particularly high—that is India, Developing Asia, and North Africa and the Middle East.

Combining the number of women of childbearing age with their propensity to have a child gives the expected number of total births. This indicates that total births should decline in the future because, while the number of women of childbearing age is growing marginally, the birth rate per thousand women is generally declining. In 2012, total births are estimated at 89.8 million and, by 2032, this is projected to decline to 81.1 million, a 10 percent absolute decline and a factor that will slow overall population growth in the years to 2032. As shown in Figure 2.2, the majority of these births will continue to be in India, Developing Asia, and North Africa and the Middle East.

The biggest determinants of how many children a couple has are education and affluence.

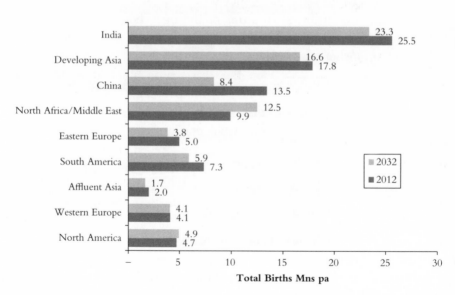

Figure 2.2 Total Births (Millions per Year) by Region, 2012 and 2032
Source: Global Demographics Ltd.

An interesting question is, what could change this prediction? The only factor that can really change over the next 20 years is the propensity of women to have a child. The number of girls that are alive today determines the number of women of childbearing age in 2032 with some certainty. The propensity to have a child is potentially more variable but historically it has followed a steady (declining) trend in line with improvements in education and affluence. The projected improvements in education and affluence indicate that this downward trend in propensity to have a child is expected to continue, but there is the possible exception that in difficult economic times better-educated adults may opt to have even fewer children to ensure that these children are provided for. So, the area of uncertainty in this scenario is at the lower end—that is, slightly fewer births may result from current and future economic challenges.

What about China and India?

With respect to China there are two issues in relation to births. The first is the impact of the one-child policy if it is not continued. The second is the gender bias of births. In terms of the one-child policy, there is a frequently expressed perception that if it were to be relaxed there would be a significant increase in the Chinese birth rate.

China's one-child policy and its implications are frequently misunderstood; the policy currently applies to only about 38 percent of households.

For that reason alone it is useful to briefly examine the one-child policy, which may not be properly understood. First, the one-child policy mainly applies to people who were registered at birth as being urban dwellers. The constraints on rural households are less severe. When the policy was introduced, only about 30 percent of the population was urban based, increasing to 38 percent in 1990, which effectively determines the proportion of adults of childbearing age today that are constrained by this policy (i.e., those born in an urban area and now of childbearing age). The rest of the population can have a second child, even those who have subsequently migrated from rural to urban areas. However, for those who can have more than one child, they have to pay for the health care and education expenses of all their children if they have moved from their rural village where they are registered (*haiku*) to an urban area, and this acts as an effective constraint on these people's desire to have more than one child.

Concerning whether the Chinese government will relax the policy, it should be appreciated that under the one-child policy, two adults who are both from a one-child family are themselves exempt. This clause has had little effect over the last 20 years, as until now very few married couples were the product of the one-child legislation. However, this is starting to change as, increasingly, those having children today in urban areas are both from one-child families, so they can have more than one child if they wish. The question is, "Will they?"

Increasingly, the biggest determinants of how many children a couple has, whether in China or elsewhere, are the education and affluence of the potential parents. As these variables increase in a society, that society's propensity to have children is lowered. Singapore is an example of this. It, therefore, seems likely that the increasing affluence and rising educational standards in China will generally inhibit the propensity to have more than one child. So overall the impact of the one-child policy is low and its relaxation would have little impact on the current course of population growth.

The other issue in terms of births in China is the gender bias to males. The latest detailed data on births are for 2010 (from the census done in that year), which indicate that for every 100 females born, 126 males are born. This is a very high imbalance. For example, of the 13.69 million babies born in 2010, 7.67 million are boys and 6.016 are girls. What is more, the data indicate that this ratio has not decreased over the last decade in spite of increased education, urbanisation, and potentially less traditionalism. Its impact will hit home in the next 20 years. For example, in 2032, there will be around 29 million more males of marrying age (20 to 39 years of age) than there are females. This represents a shortfall of around 18 percent in terms of females. Collectively between 2012 and 2032 it is estimated that there will be 40 million males who cannot get married because of the shortage of marriageable aged females. The social implications of this could be considerable.

India is different. As there has been no constraint on having children, the number of births per thousand females of childbearing age has been much higher than that of China (and most other countries as well). Even in 2012, the birth rate per thousand Indian women of childbearing age is estimated at 83, compared with 38 in China. The birth rate in India is expected to continue to decline, as education standards increase, assisted by government policies and education programs highlighting the benefits of contraception. The forecast model—driven by projected trends in the education profile of adults and average household income—indicates that the birth rate in India will decline from 83 per thousand women of childbearing age in 2012 to 63 in 2032, a significant reduction. However, India's problem is that this decline in the propensity to have children is more than offset by the unavoidable growth in the number of women of childbearing age, as detailed in the previous section of this chapter. It is unavoidable because the majority of these women are already alive as children today. As shown earlier in Table 2.1, the number of women of childbearing age is expected to increase from 306 million in 2012 to reach 373 million in 2032. This is a 22 percent absolute increase.

In 2012, the birth rate per thousand Indian women of childbearing age was 84, compared with 37 in China. In the years to 2032, India's population will grow every year by slightly more than the total population of the Netherlands or Chile.

As a result, total births in India in 2012 will be an estimated 25.5 million. By 2032 it is estimated to have declined only marginally to 23.3 million, meaning that after allowing for deaths, India's population will have natural growth (that is excluding the effects of migration) every year by slightly more than 17.4 million persons—which is about the same as the total population of the Netherlands or Chile. Clearly, a more aggressive reduction in the birth rate would lower that further, but it is already forecast to decline by a third. Can a steeper drop, which is clearly desirable sociologically, be achieved? In comparison, China's total births in 2012 are expected to be 13.5 million and by 2032 are projected to be 8.4 million.

Switching to the global view, the total number of people being born in 2032 will be 8.7 million less per annum than it is today, and newborns as a percentage of total population will drop from 1.6 percent to 1.3 percent. This leads us to the second part of the equation concerning overall population growth: What is happening to the number of deaths?

Death Rates

When looking at deaths, it is important to appreciate the difference between the average death rate, and the death rate within an age group. Clearly, as death rates for persons over 40 years are higher than for those under 40 years of age, as a population gets older and the proportion of people over the age of 40 increases, the total number of deaths and average deaths per thousand persons in the total population also rises. However, within an individual age group (for example persons aged 60 to 64 years), for virtually every country in the world, and certainly all those included in our study, the death rate is typically declining. This reflects improved nutrition, better primary health care, and better medicine. So the increase in total deaths over the next two decades is a function of the ageing of the global population rather than declining health standards.

As with birth rates, death rates by age and by gender show steady and consistent trends over time. Again, this varies between countries but within a particular country, age or gender, there is very little variation from the trend. It would take a catastrophic epidemic for this to change. Even SARS is not detectable in the overall trend of death rates for Hong Kong. Given that we know the existing age profile of the population by gender, and we have good data on the trend of death rates by age and gender over time, we can with quite high reliability estimate the number of deaths for each year through to 2032, as shown in Figure 2.3.

The bad news is that the total number of deaths is projected to increase significantly. However, as explained, this increase is a function of having more old people, rather than a reduction in life expectancy. Total deaths in 2012 are estimated at 36.1 million. By 2032, the increasing size of the older population will more than offset the declines in death rates within age groups, so that total deaths reach 51.9 million. Death is clearly a growth industry.

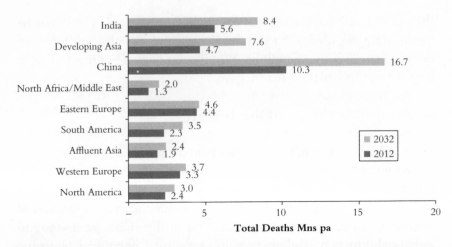

Figure 2.3 Total Deaths (Millions per Year) by Region/Country 2012 and 2032

The Implications for Total Population Changes

The next questions that arise are: What do these trends in births and deaths mean for the total population of each region, and what are the implications of the continuing migration trends of the last five years? Starting with natural population change (i.e., excluding for the moment migration) if the number of deaths exceeds the number of births, then the natural change in the population would, of course, be negative. In 2012, no region had more deaths than births, so everywhere was experiencing some growth as a result of natural population change (remember, migration is not included in this particular stage of the analysis). However some individual countries in Eastern and Western Europe, as well as Japan, already have negative natural growth, and these regions, as well as China, are experiencing relatively low natural population growth. In contrast, India, Developing Asia, North Africa, the Middle East, South America and North America are all experiencing high natural population growth.

However, in 20 years, there is a very different picture. The forecast model suggests Eastern Europe and Affluent Asia will move into negative natural population growth, and that Western Europe will approach this point. In China, the natural, population growth rate in 2032 will be significantly negative: China's total population will peak in 2018 and decline thereafter. As a result, by 2024 the model suggests that India will have a larger population than China.

As highlighted at the start of this chapter, population growth has come to be seen as almost inexorable. More people result in even more people, while improvements in health care (the focus of Chapter 9) are having a major impact by

By 2024 the model predicts that India will have a larger population than China.

extending life spans. However, there is a shift happening, a number of countries and ultimately regions covered in this book are moving to stable or ultimately declining total populations. At present (with the exception of China) they account for a relatively small proportion of the total population of the world and as such are not slowing global population growth very much. China will have a bigger impact and over time the global trend may become neutral, which has to be good for the world.

In addition to these natural population changes, migration also needs to be factored in. As mentioned, the model uses the trend by age and gender for the previous five years for forecasting. This, of course, assumes there is no change in government immigration policy by those countries which tend to be important in terms of immigration as opposed to emigration. This includes the United States, Canada, Australia, Singapore, and the more affluent regions of Western Europe, as basically immigration follows money. Few people move to a country where they might be worse off.

Subject to the uncertainty of immigration trends, but using the solidarity of birth and death rates, Table 2.2 summarises the likely changes in total population by region over the next 20 years.

The first point to note is that China, Eastern Europe, and Affluent Asia are all projected to have negative population growth in the years to 2032, mostly happening after 2022. Also, the majority of the population change (and, as it happens, growth) will come from India and Developing Asia, and within that region in particular from Pakistan and Bangladesh. Clearly attention should also be drawn to the almost

Table 2.2 Changes in Total Population by Region/Country (2012–2032)

	Total Population (Millions)		Change (Millions)	CAGR 2012 to 2032
	2012	2032		
North America	351	415	64	0.8%
Western Europe	412	437	25	0.3%
Affluent Asia	239	232	−7	−0.1%
South America	476	549	72	0.7%
Eastern Europe	405	396	−9	−0.1%
North Africa/ Middle East	380	545	165	1.8%
China	1,348	1,297	−51	−0.2%
Developing Asia	876	1,070	194	1.0%
India	1,192	1,446	253	1.0%
Total	5,680	6,386	706	0.4%

SOURCE: Global Demographics Ltd.

explosive population growth of North Africa and the Middle East (projected to average 1.8 percent per annum).

These trends will affect the share of the world population accounted for by each region, and Figure 2.4 shows that the older, affluent countries largely maintain their share as does South America and Eastern Europe. Conversely, North Africa and the Middle East, Developing Asia, and India will all increase their share of population by one or two percentage points. In contrast, China is projected to decline from being 24 percent of the population of the 74 countries in this study, to 20 percent by 2032. This decline in share will be a function of population growth elsewhere, as well as a drop in China's total population.

The Changing Age Profile

While each region's position, in terms of share of total population, will remain relatively constant, there are some dramatic changes expected in the global age profile by 2032 and these are highlighted in Figure 2.5. Globally, the 0 to 14 age group declines by 61 million

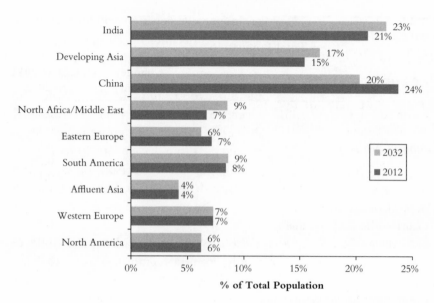

Figure 2.4 Projected Changes in Share of Global Population 2012–2032
Source: Global Demographics Ltd.

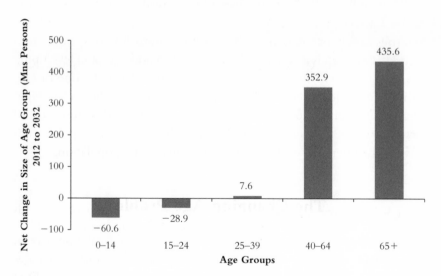

Figure 2.5 Global Changes in the Size of Age Groups: 2012–2032
Source: Global Demographics Ltd.

On a global basis, between 2012 and 2032 the only age groups to increase in size are those over the age of 40 years. The youth segments are now in absolute decline in size.

(a 4.6 percent decline) while the 15 to 24 age group declines by 29 million and the 25 to 39 year age group is on the cusp of this significant change in the age profile of the world and shows virtually no change in absolute number over the next 20 years. Clearly, the growth age groups for the next two decades are 40 to 64 years (adding 353 million persons or 21 percent to its 2012 size) and 65+ (adding 436 million or 81 percent), as the baby boomer population bulge moves into middle and old age.

This has implications for the demand and market positioning of various products. To put it bluntly, in most regions (and countries) the child and youth market faces a declining number of consumers, whereas the mature adult market will see growth. Yet how many products or services target this group?

There are, however, several notable differences between countries and regions by age group, as shown in Table 2.3. For instance, the number of children defined as those under 14 years of age is still growing in North Africa and the Middle East and, marginally, in developing Asia

Table 2.3 Absolute Change in Each Age Group (in Millions of People), 2012 to 2032

	0–14	15–24	25–39	40–64	65+
North America	6.6	3.0	9.3	6.1	38.6
Western Europe	−1.1	−0.8	−5.7	−5.7	38.8
Affluent Asia	−7.4	−6.5	−10.5	−2.4	19.8
South America	−17.8	−5.2	−4.3	59.7	39.8
Eastern Europe	−9.5	−5.6	−27.7	12.2	21.5
North Africa/Middle East	37.1	24.3	23.5	60.2	20.0
China	−68.0	−54.9	−62.1	−20.3	154.2
Developing Asia	6.0	−0.6	20.1	118.1	50.6
India	−6.4	17.4	65.0	125.1	52.4
Total	−60.6	−28.9	7.6	352.9	435.6

SOURCE: Global Demographics Ltd.

and North America. This contrasts with the declining size of this age group in all other regions. Once again, the change in China is particularly notable, as the number of children is projected to decline by 68 million in the next two decades, a reduction of 32 percent. Clearly, the Chinese child market may be large but it is declining, a situation with important implications for anyone selling to this group. It seems likely that with respect to this market segment, the marketing challenges will be to keep customer loyalty and increase revenue per customer as the target market itself is declining in absolute number.

The next point to note is that the overall trend is for societies to age, with countries finding that more of their population is in the older segments. The 40 to 65 year segment, which is the lucrative working age empty nester age group, is projected to increase by 353 million persons in 20 years, a 21 percent increase over 20 years. This group is of particular importance as they are very able consumers. This is typically a household in which the children have grown up and left home and, as such, the household has fewer dependents. In many countries with a good history of education these households have more than one earner as the spouse who looked after the children is increasingly more likely to return to the workforce by this stage.

This reduction in number of dependents means that discretionary incomes of these households increases dramatically and that, in turn, has implications for the consumer markets where this age group is significant. This is typically the older (and more affluent) countries and regions, as shown in Figure 1.3. Yet there are relatively few brands or products/services currently targeting this group overtly. Rather, the mantra is to target the young middle class in India and China, with a complete unawareness that the young are not the growth segments in these countries (nor are they higher earners).

Finally, the 65+ age group is expected to grow by nearly 2 percent per annum or more in every region. This group has significantly higher demands on health care, pensions, and other financial services, which cannot be ignored. However, it is also a significant market opportunity for many products and services. It is perhaps

By 2032 nearly one in three of all people in the countries covered in this book aged 65 and above will be in China.

worth noting that whereas many regard China as a youth market, this perception is mistaken. Already 27 percent of the world's population over the age of 64 is in China and by 2032 it will be 31 percent. To put it in another way, by 2032 nearly one in three of all people in the countries covered in this book aged 65 and above will be in China. Furthermore, the 65 years and above age group will have increased from being 9 percent of the global population to 15 percent, and 4 out of 10 of them will be in either China or India. It might also be noted that the consumption power of this segment is increasing. In the affluent regions they are working longer, and have more savings than earlier generations.

Summary

The key message is that future population growth is greatly influenced by the world's current age profile. The proportion of the population that is of childbearing age significantly determines the future number of births and, conversely, the proportion of the population over 64 significantly impacts on total deaths. With their very young populations total population growth is now biased towards India, Developing Asia, and the Middle East/North Africa. The good news is that the rate of population growth in these parts of the world is slowing, but perhaps not swiftly enough to prevent major social, political, and economic shocks. This makes these regions disproportionately more important.

Interestingly, while age profile is a key determinant of the future size of the total population, one of the most dramatic changes in the next 20 years will be in the shape of the age profile. After decades of growth, the number of young people worldwide is either flat or declining. The population segments that are growing in the future are aged over 40, and these people are particularly attractive as consumer markets, as we will see later in Chapter 8.

It is worth observing the position of South America in terms of this. It is very much in the transit, being some way away from those countries that are young and have still growing young populations, but also while ageing; it is biased still to the 40 to 64 age range rather than the 65-plus age group as is the older countries. It will become the middle aged of the world.

Finally, the implications of the growth of the over-65 population is already being felt, with societies coming to terms with the fact that there are more people in this age group than ever before and they living longer. As a proportion of the global population they increase from 9 percent to 15 percent; in absolute number they increase by 435 million in 20 years, and one in three of them will be in China.

This changing age structure of the populations of the world has implications beyond births and deaths. It also impacts the actual structure of the household as well the size and trend in the labour force. These issues are examined in the subsequent chapters.

Chapter 3

Tomorrow's Household

How many households are there in the world? How are they changing, how many people are in each household—and why does it matter? So many of the decisions that we make, from what to buy to how we choose to spend our time, result from one or two very simple facts: how many people live in our household and their age profile. As a result, the number of households, and perhaps more importantly the life-cycle stage of those households, has a significant impact on the current and future demand for products and services.

The Modern Household

Although one might expect the total number of households to grow at a similar rate to the population, this is only the case if the number of people per household remains constant—and it doesn't. What we are finding is that just as birth and death rates are changing, along

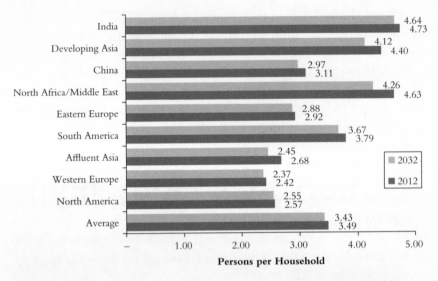

Figure 3.1 Average Number of People per Household, 2012 and 2032
Source: Global Demographics Ltd.

To predict the market-place of the future we need to look close to home. The household is particularly important to our understanding of demand because, as a unit, it affects so many fundamental decisions about what we buy and our total pattern of consumption. In fact, households are the decision unit for many consumer purchases.

with educational standards, employment opportunities, and attitudes to a range of issues, so too is the composition of the typical home.

Globally, the average number of people per household is 3.49, as shown in Figure 3.1. There are relatively few regions that have an average of more than four people in a household and, unsurprisingly, they tend to be in the younger, less-educated regions of the world with higher than average birth rates, including India, Developing Asia, North Africa. All of these regions have an average household size of 4.4 or more persons. Given the younger age profile, this means that the typical household in these regions has two adults and two or more children. This will undoubtedly affect spending and saving patterns in these areas.

Average households in the younger regions of the world contrast sharply with the situation prevailing in the affluent, older regions, where the average household size is significantly less than three. In 2012, Western Europe has the lowest average household size with 2.4 people. This was followed by North America and Affluent Asia, with 2.6 and 2.7 people, respectively. Significantly, Eastern Europe and China, while not affluent, are both old and so tend to have fewer children in their households with consequent implications for household size—specifically, an average of close to three persons. South America (being the new middle aged) has a household size between the young poor and the older affluent. In South America, the average household size is 3.8 persons and expected to decline only slightly over the next two decades as the majority of the households are still family households, although increasingly reaching the stage of empty nesters by 2032.

One global trend is particularly clear: With the earlier discussed ageing of the population, average household size has been declining in every region for the last decade. By 2032, the greatest decline is expected to be in North Africa and the Middle East, where the average household size will fall by −0.4 people, closely followed by Developing Asia at −0.3 people. This is a result of the average family household having fewer children. In the older countries, the general decline that is expected in household size will be significantly a function of the growth

Average household size has been declining in every region for the last decade—a trend that is expected to continue in those older parts of the world where the number of young people is flat or declining.

in the proportion (and number) of households that become empty nester households.

Before we look at how the internal structure of the household is changing, it is useful to first understand the regional impact of a growing population coupled with a reducing household size. This matters because, as said at the beginning of this chapter, households are the decision unit for many consumer purchases. At present, there are 1.63 billion households in the 74 countries covered in this book. By 2032, this is expected to have grown by an additional 240 million households to 1.86 billion. This is an annual growth rate of 0.7 percent, or 12 million extra households every year for the next 20 years. The number of households will grow particularly rapidly in North Africa and the Middle East. The population in these regions is projected to grow at 1.8 percent per annum and the average household size is projected to decline by 0.4 percent per annum. As a result, the number of households in this region is projected to grow at 2.25 percent per annum, taking it from 82 million to 127 million households by 2032. This is a 56 percent increase, a fact that will have significant implications for the consumer markets in those areas as well as the construction industry.

The more affluent regions of the world will create 46 million new households, a growth rate of just 0.5 percent per annum. However, North America, with a growing population and a slightly slower decline in household size (owing to its younger population), is growing its number of households at just under 1 percent per annum. As shown in Figure 3.2, between 2012 and 2032, the number of households in these affluent regions will increase from 396 million to 441 million, an additional two million households every year.

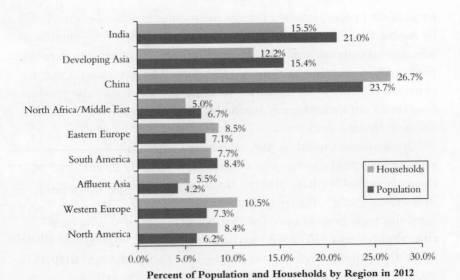

Percent of Population and Households by Region in 2012

Figure 3.2 Percentage of Population and Households by Region in 2012
Source: Global Demographics Ltd.

While the affluent regions account for nearly 18 percent of the total population, they account for 24 percent, or one in four, of all households. This makes these regions disproportionately more important than their population alone would suggest, as households are the ultimate decision unit. In contrast, India, with its current average household size of 4.7 people, has a large percentage of the world's population (21 percent), but with 252 million households, it only has 15 percent of the world's households. It is interesting to compare this to China, which has an average household size of 3.1 persons. China with 1.35 billion people has 433 million households. This is a significant difference in terms of the number of decision units (households). Because of its large population and relatively small household size, China accounts for 27 percent of all households in the countries covered.

The Changing Nature of Tomorrow's Households

In addition to the projected change in absolute number of households by region, there are also changes taking place in terms of the number of persons in the household and their age profile, all of which affect the potential consumption patterns of the future. The key changes that are expected to emerge include the emerging dominance of the childless household and the changing number of dependents per wage earner in the household.

A significant trend is the increasing number of childless homes, defined as those households that contain no one under the age of 19. It may be surprising to note the high proportion of such homes that already exist. In 2012, two out of every five households have no child—by 2032, this is expected to increase to nearly one in two households. In fact, the number of childless households is projected to increase from 659 million to

In 2012, two out of every five households have no child—by 2032, this is expected to increase to nearly one in two households.

873 million, an increase of 213 million by 2032. Again, the implications for consumer demand and product marketing are significant.

A childless household typically (but not exclusively) comprises two adults over the age of 40, of whom at least one is a wage earner in those households in which the adults are still under retirement age. This means a very low dependency ratio and higher per capita discretionary funds. To gain an insight of the impact of this, consider Western Europe, where the average childless household contains 1.66 people compared with the 3.95 people in households containing children. Assuming that each household has an average income of US$80,000 per annum, the household with children has a per capita income of US$20,253 per annum, compared with US$48,192 for the childless households. Such a discrepancy will have an enormous influence on what each household will want and be able to buy as well as ability to save. This extra US$28,000 per capita to spend (US$48,192– US$20,253) is probably mainly discretionary money and, as such, this shift in the bias of households to smaller childless ones will be a major driver for the growth of discretionary spending, that is, recreation, travel, health care or wellness, eating out, and so on. This is a shift from things which they already have plenty of in the more affluent regions, to experiences. In fact, it may well be a surprise to many consumer product and service marketers that the new opportunity is not young adults but, rather, older adults, in that the latter are growing in number and have greater aggregate discretionary money, and this segment in the affluent countries are well-educated, technologically competent, able consumers.

Figure 3.3 highlights the global pattern of childless households and reveals several interesting differences among regions. In Affluent Asia and Western Europe, two out of every three households already have no children in them. By 2032, this is projected to increase to nearly three out of every four households. This translates into an additional 30 million households whose lifestyle and consumption profile are projected to change significantly over the next two decades. There is expected to be an 18 percent increase in the size of this segment (whereas the number of households with children shrinks by 10 million—or 12 percent—over the same period).

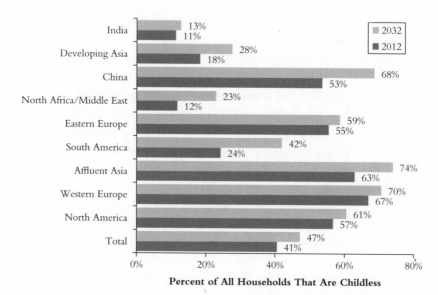

Figure 3.3 Estimated Proportion of All Households That Are Childless, 2012 and 2032
Source: Global Demographics Ltd.

Currently, 53 percent of households in China are childless; this is projected to reach nearly 68 percent of households by 2032. This move in China to the 1.5 wage earner household with no children helps explain the rapid growth of discretionary spending in this consumer market in recent years and, given the forecast in terms of these variables, this market growth will continue for the next two decades. This has implications for many market segments but particularly those such as personal care, travel, recreation, and entertainment.

The situation in China stands in marked contrast with India. In India, nine out of ten households include a child. As shown earlier, a reduction in the number of children in a household, when coupled with an increase in disposable income, has an enormous (almost exponential) impact on people's ability to consume. Clearly that cannot be expected to happen in India where the proportion of households with at least one child in them remains at 89 percent for the next two decades. This means the number of dependents per worker is high and reduces the ability of the Indian household to save or engage in more discretionary expenditure. The booming middle class household that many refer to in India (see Chapter 7) may be large in number but is actually small in spending power per person and, hence, potentially not a good profit opportunity.

Of the countries with relatively low incidence of childless households in 2012, all but India will experience significant increases in proportion and number by 2032. South America, North Africa and the Middle East, and Developing Asia all nearly double in incidence of childless households over the next two decades, indicating that the empty nester household is a growth segment.

Employment and Dependency Ratios

The growing incidence of childless households and, hence, greater discretionary funds, however, is just one way that the changing nature of households are potentially shaping the future. The twin issues of employment and dependency ratios are also significant. The number of people in a household that are in paid employment determines its

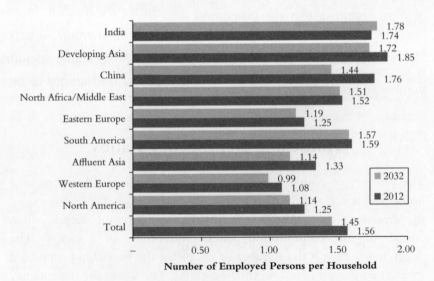

Figure 3.4 Average Number of Employed Persons per Household 2012 and 2032
Source: Global Demographics Ltd.

ability to earn and, as a result, affects that household's spending power and ability to save. Figure 3.4 shows the relative number of employed persons per household by region, and this does differ significantly across regions. It should also be noted that there is a slight inverse relationship between earnings and number of employed persons. In a low-income country, the pressure for as many people as possible in the household to be employed is high, whereas in a high-income country there is the option for some members of the household not to be in paid employment as the earnings of (typically) one person are sufficient to cover the needs of the household. This is perhaps why the number of earners per household is significantly lower in the more affluent regions. It also reflects the fact that the less affluent regions tend to have their young adults working even though they are still in the family home. In the affluent regions the equivalent age group is still in school.

Overall, it is projected to have relatively little change in the number of earners per household over time. As discussed in Chapter 5 on labour force, such is the stability in the propensity to be employed of most countries that the proportion of the population employed tends to move in line with number of adults, which, in turn, is the most significant determinant of the number of households.

The number of people in a household that are in paid employment determines its absolute income and, as a result, affects that household's spending power and ability to save.

Household Dependency Ratios

The number of employed people in each household relative to total household size (total number of persons in the household) determines the *dependency ratio*, which is a particularly important statistic when considering the consumption pattern and power of a society. The dependency ratio is the number of people in the household supported by each employed person in the household. The lower the dependency ratio, the greater is the household's ability either to save or to engage in more discretionary spending, or both. Figure 3.5 compares the average

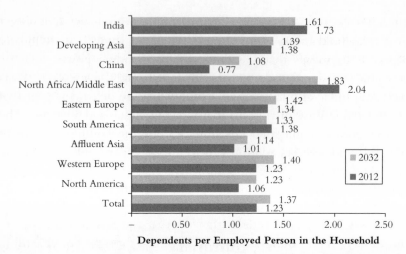

Figure 3.5 Average Number of Dependents per Employed Person in Each Household, 2012 and 2032
Source: Global Demographics Ltd.

number of dependents per employed person in each household for each region in 2012 and as forecast for 2032.

Clearly, China is slightly out of step with the rest of the world. At 0.71 dependents per employed person per household, China has one of the lowest dependency ratios in the world, which has been a significant factor behind the increased consumer spending that has been taking place in the last few years. The continuing decline in the birth rate and total births in recent decades, combined with a disproportionately high number of working-age people with a high propensity to be employed, has resulted in an average household with 1.8 workers and just over 1.3 nonworkers (child or older adult) per household. This means that the average worker in China is supporting 1.77 people—themselves and 0.77 of another person. However, do note how the age bias of the population (increasingly to persons over the age of 40 years) is affecting this dependency ratio over the next decade. By 2032, the ratio will be a more normal 1.08 dependents per worker, and that might be expected to have some impact on the propensity to both save and spend.

Despite their older populations, developed countries nonetheless have low dependency ratios. At present, Affluent Asia and North

America have around one dependent person for every employed worker in the household and Western Europe has 1.2. As we will discuss in later chapters, this means that the discretionary spending power of these households is significantly enhanced. Interestingly, Developing Asia (excluding India) also has a reasonably low average dependency ratio of 1.4—reflecting the situation in Thailand, Indonesia, and Vietnam. The key exceptions, highlighted in Figure 3.5, are the youthful regions of India, the Middle East and North Africa. In these parts of the world, the average working person is supporting typically 1.6 to 2.0 other people in the home. However, in both cases the ratio will decline significantly over the next two decades.

Summary

Because it is the principal decision unit for much of our consumption, the future nature of the household is vital to our understanding of consumption trends. One global trend that is particularly important in respect of households is towards fewer people (particularly dependent children) per household. Because this is happening at the same time as the population is increasing, the absolute number of households will rise at a faster rate than the general population. As a result, while the number of consumers is rising, the number of key decision units (households) is increasing even faster.

In 2012 the average household has 3.5 persons in it, and trends in births, marrying age, and overall age profile of the population indicate that this will decline marginally over the next two decades. But the affluent regions with their older population already have a significantly lower average household size than the poor regions.

While a 20-year boom in the number of households worldwide is significant enough, it is really at the micro level where the implications of this change are best understood and managed. Because an increasing proportion of households will lack anyone at all under the age of 18, they will be adult households. This change will have a significant impact on future patterns of consumption.

In the years to 2032, households will also change in another meaningful way: how many of their members are employed. This affects the per capita income of the household and its ability to save and to engage in discretionary spending. Overall, the number of dependents in the household relative to the number of workers will increase in the more affluent regions and decline in the less affluent regions. However, China and Eastern Europe, with their older but poor populations, will be an exception to this trend. The combination of ageing (entering retirement) and affluence (thereby less need for both adults to be employed) will see the number of dependents per worker increase over time.

Next, we will address some of the most interesting changes and pressing challenges resulting from changing demography in the next chapter: education, capital, and productivity.

Chapter 4

Education and Productivity

Education matters at every level of society. Educated individuals are likely to earn more and have more options for their life and career; an intelligent and skilled workforce is likely to be more competitive and commercially successful. Education also significantly impacts on how demography affects the world in which we live, such as birth rates, attitudes toward healthier lifestyles, and hygiene. Social progress will only take place when the population is educated and able to work productively.

Clearly, the extent of a nation's education system profoundly affects how its people think and act, but the first general point is that there is a time lag between cause and effect, often with a significant delay between investments in learning and the resulting changes in society or developments in lifestyle. For example, there is an inverse relationship between the level of education and the number of children that people choose to have, which is only apparent when the generation benefiting from changes in education mature to childbearing age. Similarly, there is a positive relationship between education and productivity in the workforce, a factor that drives wages, household income and consumption—but, again, there is a time delay between being educated and being in the workforce and productive. It should also be remembered that demographic change can also easily threaten educational standards. If a population's growth exceeds its investment in education, then standards will decline, which, in turn, reduces the productivity of the population and its ability to continue to invest in education. It can become a vicious cycle. This chapter explores the relationship between these forces in greater detail.

One of the biggest issues affecting a nation's future is the provision of education, and this is why it is so important to accurately measure and understand each country's current state of education and likely future trends.

Understanding education levels is not a straightforward task: It is notoriously difficult both to measure and to make comparisons between countries, a challenge that is complicated by the many different definitions and criteria that each society uses. Despite these difficulties, it is necessary to understand the facts behind demography and education so that governments, businesses, and individuals can make the best decisions.

The Education Index

Faced with the challenge of measuring something that is difficult to assess but too important to ignore, an index was devised that simply reflects the likely number of years in education for the average adult in the workforce in each country weighted upwards for more years (for example, the extra years spent doing a vocational qualification carry 50 percent more weight than years at secondary stage). The longer the average time spent in education and the higher the achievement, the higher the index value. This is designed to overcome the fact that primary, secondary, and tertiary education start at different ages and are often of varying duration in different countries, while being relatively robust and easy to understand.

The best-educated regions are North America, Affluent Asia, and Western Europe, while the countries with the biggest challenges educationally are India and the countries of North Africa and the Middle East.

Figure 4.1 compares regions according to their indexed score. The average for all 59 countries covered in this analysis for which education data are available is 177, ranging from 91 for India to a maximum of 269 for North America. As one would expect, the best-educated regions are North America, Affluent Asia, and Western Europe, while the countries with the biggest challenges educationally are India and the countries of North Africa and the Middle East.

Fortunately, the march of progress and the emphasis placed on education worldwide means that the values in the education index are expected to improve in the future; the rate of improvement, however, varies significantly by region and country. Figure 4.1 highlights the fact that the range in improvement is projected to vary from 57 percent for

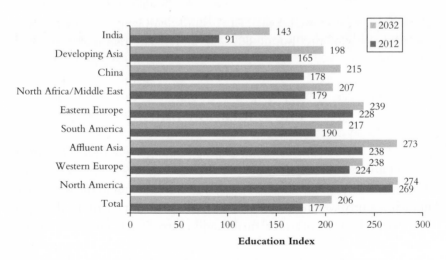

Figure 4.1 Relative Education Index by Region, 2012 and 2032
Source: Global Demographics Ltd.

India, 21 percent for China, and 20 percent for Developing Asia to 2 percent for North America. Several factors cause this variation, including number of new entrants into adult age (older societies have a lower proportion entering adulthood in any one year), the existing overall educational profile of the adult population, and, of course, improvements being achieved in education facilities (easier for countries with poor systems now than for countries with a history of good education facilities). Not surprisingly, Japan, for example, cannot improve its overall education score very much. It already has a high score, the existing quality of education services is high, and there are relatively (compared with the total adult population) few persons exiting the good standard education system and impacting the overall standard of average education score of all adults. In contrast, India is in the process of improving its education facilities and their availability and has a large number of people exiting the education system and entering the adult population, with a significantly better standard of education than the existing adult population.

The fact that the index (and perceived education standard of the adult population) is improving in the regions where it is currently low is good news for the world. It will lift the ability of those people to be productive and earn an income which supports a good lifestyle. Based on behavioural patterns elsewhere in the world, there are also reasonable grounds to expect that it will result in lower birth rates and greater social stability. Finally, it should be noted here that the forecast values are based on the trend in the enrolment profile of children in each country—that is, the proportion (and number) that is receiving education to a certain number of years. This in turn provides a good estimate of the education profile of those exiting the education system each year and the impact of that on the overall average profile of adults.

Later in this chapter we will address the implications of different values on the education index for a country's development, but initially it is important to look at factors that inhibit or encourage the improvement of the overall education standard.

The Future Demand for Education (and Standards)

One factor that significantly impacts the ability of a country to lift (or even maintain) its education standard is the future demand for education and educational facilities. Typically, the lower the demand for schools, the greater the quality of education that can be supplied. (This relies, of course, on all other things being equal, such as investments in education, teacher numbers, and other resources.) A good measure of the level of demand is the trend in the number of primary school-age children that are expected in future, that is, children aged from 6 to 11 years, inclusive. Rather than looking at the absolute number of primary school children that can be expected—a figure which is dominated by the youth in India and, to a lesser extent, China—it is better to simply examine the percentage change in the number of children requiring a primary education in the years from 2012 to 2032, which is shown in Figure 4.2. When we do this, what becomes clear is the fact that, with the exception of the Middle East and North Africa, North America, and Developing Asia, the total demand for primary education is in decline.

With the exception of the Middle East and North Africa, North America, and Developing Asia, the total demand for primary education is in decline.

This is actually good news, as it means that the same resources are being applied to fewer people, hopefully resulting in an upgrade in the

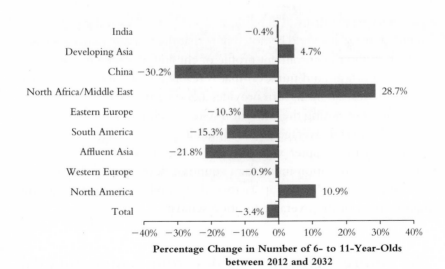

Figure 4.2   Projected Changes in Demand for Primary School Education, 2012–2032
Source: Global Demographics Ltd.

overall educational experience, as well as making higher-level education more affordable for society—that is, resources (particularly financial resources) allocated to primary education can be shifted to providing/ enabling vocational and tertiary level education. In particular, it's worth noting the dramatic decline in demand that is occurring in China and Affluent Asia. The lack of growth of demand in India is also good news, as lifting the education standard of the next generation is a critical factor to its future success, if not survival.

Another factor affecting the overall educational profile of the adult population and its wider impact on society is the proportion of the future workforce that is composed of recent graduates of the education system. These people are typically much better educated than older members of the adult population, as a result of increasing and improving education facilities over time. Figure 4.3 shows the proportion of working age in 2032 that became working age since 2012.

For the older regions of Affluent Asia, Western Europe, North America, Eastern Europe, and China, only 29 percent to 38 percent of the working age population in 2032 will have entered it in the

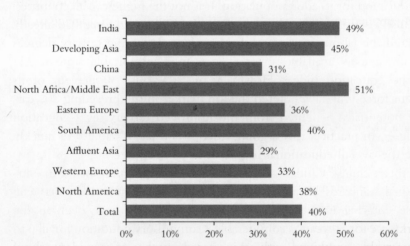

Proportion of 2032 Working-age Population That Become Working Age after 2012

Figure 4.3 Proportion of 2032 Working-age Population That Will Have Joined It Since 2012
Source: Global Demographics Ltd.

preceding 20 years (since 2012). This compares with 51 percent in North Africa and the Middle East, 45 percent in Developing Asia, and 49 percent in India. This is why it is so critical that these younger regions get their education system working now. If they don't, then over half their future labour force will lack the necessary skills to survive in a modern world, where many unskilled jobs are being performed by robots. This, in turn, will mean their economies will stagnate. Clearly, the stakes are high and the opportunity to make further educational, economic, and social progress in these regions is huge: To put it bluntly, nearly one out of every two people in their workforce in 2032 will be someone who might benefit from an investment in education by this country today.

In India and Developing Asia, nearly one out of every two people in their workforce in 2032 will be someone who might benefit from an investment in education by their country today. To delay education investment will be an opportunity lost.

Compare this scenario with Japan. Japan already has a good standard of education for its adult population. It is not the highest of all countries, because a significant proportion of the Japanese workforce had already entered the labour market by the time vocational and tertiary degrees became widely available; even so, it is in a comfortable zone at 224 in the education index. However, by 2032 just 30 percent of its labour force will have entered the job market in the preceding 20 years and potentially benefited from the improved tertiary-level education facilities. In practice, this is going to constrain Japan's ability to quickly raise the overall educational profile of its labour force.

Interestingly, China is expected to achieve a significant lift in educational standards because the gap in education attainment between those entering employment now and those who have been in the workforce for 20 years is considerable. Compulsory education for all 6 to 12 year olds, combined with an increased number of secondary school resources and vocational facilities, means that the difference between the new entrants and existing members of the workforce is considerable. So, while the proportion of the Chinese labour force in 2032 that will have been new entrants between 2012 and 2032 is just 31 percent, the difference in educational standards provided by this 31 percent (which in absolute terms is also a large number of workers) means that they will give a very significant boost to the overall educational profile of China's labour force.

Education's Impact on Society

We mentioned earlier that education is important because it has a tangible relationship with several crucial economic variables. In particular, it has a clear relationship with the propensity to have children, to attract capital, and to improve productivity. The nature of these relationships will be examined further in this section.

Education and the Birth Rate

Leaving aside the issue of what causes what, there is undoubtedly a strong inverse relationship between the level of education of the adult population and the propensity to have children. Clearly, the birth rate declines as educational standards improve, until the birth rate reaches 40 births per thousand women of childbearing age. It is worth noting that the birth rate does increase for some countries with older populations because of changing attitudes and an increasing number of births by older women. However, in the younger and poor regions, the improving educational standards, especially in those societies presently with a relatively low standard of education and a high birth rate, will alter households' priorities and expectations, which will result in the declining birth rates in future years.

Education at Work: Investing in Workers and Improving Productivity

When assessing the overall impact of education, another important connection is between the quality of education and the value of the output per worker.

Figure 4.4 helps to explain the connection. While not the greatest of statistical fits, it does show how an increase in the education index in the

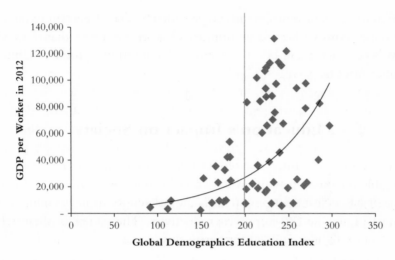

Figure 4.4 The Education Index and Productivity (Measured in GDP per Worker)
Source: Global Demographics Ltd.

range below 200 tends not to generate a proportionate increase in productivity. However, once the education index passes 200, then there is the possibility of an almost exponential lift. This is best explained anecdotally in that until 200 is reached, the level and quality of fixed capital investment per worker is probably quite low, simply because of limitations in their ability to use the equipment. However, once 200 is passed, then higher-value equipment can be provided, which in turn could lift the overall productivity of the workforce.

Do note the use of qualifiers here

Once the magic number of 200 on the education index has been achieved, there is a very high likelihood that the productivity per worker will increase rapidly and, as a result, usher in a whole new era of economic growth.

because it is evident from Figure 4.4 that improved education is a necessary but not sufficient condition to lift productivity. Many countries are past the 200 hurdle but do not have impressive productivity levels. This is a function of difficulty of investing in capital for labour to use, labour work hours, employment legislation, and so on, all of which are unique to each country.

So, the good news is that improvements in education will have a generally positive impact on productivity per worker, which, in turn, lifts household incomes and quality of life. However, the bad news is that for the many regions and countries that are currently below 200, they will not achieve significant improvements in labour force productivity in the short term. For most it will take a full two decades before they get to the 200 point on the education index simply because it takes that long for the current intake of students to get to the workforce.

But do note the position of some key economies on this scale. Brazil, Mexico, Indonesia, Thailand, Poland, Czech Republic, and China all pass the 200 mark in the next two decades. This is particularly poignant for China and Eastern Europe, as both are facing the inevitable prospect of a declining labour force. As such, the only way they can continue to grow their total economies is to lift productivity per worker at an ever faster rate. Education will enable that.

Can India Catch Up?

The situation in India warrants special attention, given the size of that country's population and its current relatively poor standard of education. Education matters for many reasons, and one of the most significant is its decisive effect on the productivity of the workforce and, as a consequence, its impact on household incomes and quality of life. The educational challenges that India faces are immense. The country currently lags behind most other countries in terms of educating its population. In 2012, there were an estimated 170 million people in India aged between 5 and 11. This is projected to decrease marginally to 169 million by 2032, reflecting the current trend of a declining birth rate. There are also an estimated 145 million Indian children currently (2012) enrolled in primary school, meaning that education was reaching 85 percent of young children. The trend of the last five years indicates that while class size may not reduce much (really, a function of ability to attract people into teaching), the coverage of 5 to 11 year olds will get close to 100 percent by 2032, which is good. It is good to see that a similar picture is emerging in terms of early secondary (up to age 16) after allowing for the proportion that have not completed primary and therefore cannot go on to secondary level.

This is a significant improvement on the situation that existed a decade ago—and given that 49 percent of India's labour force in 2032 will enter it after this year, it is a very positive indicator for overall skills of the labour force and is why India's education index is expected to improve significantly. However, the problem is that at present, only 32 percent of its workforce has more than primary education (this compares with 70 percent for China). So, even if it achieves the projected 22 million high school graduates a year between 2012 and 2032, it still means only 59 percent of its adult population will be at that level in 2032, whereas China is there already. So a definite improvement, but will it be enough? The problem is that the process cannot be accelerated—if they are largely educating the majority of children today to high school level, then that really is the best that can be done apart from also offering education to those already in the labour force.

Strategic Implications

There are two key strategic issues that flow from this chapter. The first is that education is a necessary (but not sufficient) condition to get a significant lift in productivity of workers and affluence of the population. This makes education a critical variable to watch and, for countries where the current standard of education is low, there is little to be expected in terms of increased productivity until the education system is invested in and developing and the benefits of that (better educated children) have time to flow into the workforce (i.e., working-age population). Thailand and Indonesia are two classic examples of getting this right, and one can expect their economies to grow over the next two decades at an accelerating pace, reflecting the double benefits of a growing and better educated workforce. Malaysia is an example of a country that is now past that threshold and benefiting from it.

China deserves mention here as well because as shown in the next chapter, the labour force is declining in size, and having a more productive workforce is essential to keep the total economy growing. In that respect China's timing is perfect, having reached an index value close to 178 in 2012 and a projected 195 in 2022. There are grounds for expecting increased worker productivity in those provinces of China which are actually past the 200 point, and of sufficient size to offset the impact of a declining workforce. It also, as shown later, has positive implications for the consumer market of China.

Finally, India. This is the third strategic issue that needs to be considered. India by definition is important, accounting for nearly a quarter of the world's population. However, its overall standard of education is poor, and that is inhibiting investment in the country. This is demonstrated in Figure 4.5, which compares China's and India's education profile for their adult populations. In both countries getting senior management for a business is satisfied by the proportion that has a vocational or tertiary qualification (about 7 to 10 percent). Similarly, both can find a good supply of basic workers from the 34 percent and 21 percent (India and China, respectively) who have primary education. The problem is finding the more skilled worker/middle manager. In China it is not an issue; 61 percent of working-age adults have secondary level education. In India it is a massive problem at 24 percent of working-age adults. This limits the

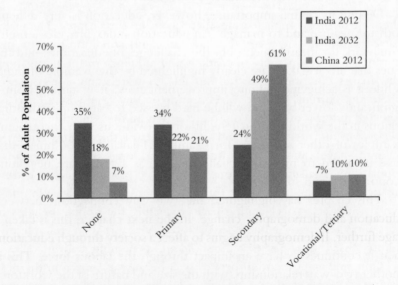

Figure 4.5 Education Profile of India and China Adults in 2012
Source: Global Demographics Ltd.

ability to operate more productive factories and causes significant wage inflation in that management/skill range.

This is why it is so important that India develops its education sector. Indications are that by 2032 India will have 49 percent of its working-age population with secondary education, which is a very significant improvement. But will the markets have waited for that to have happened, or will industrial investment have moved elsewhere by then? Indonesia, Thailand, and Eastern Europe are all better equipped now to receive this investment. As such, education is probably the most strategic aspect of demographics that one should monitor in terms of investment in India.

Summary

This chapter highlights several vital points about education and demography that are simple yet often overlooked. It matters because it affects our propensity to have children, our ability to work, the amount of money we earn, and, ultimately, our quality of life.

Despite its central importance, however, education is very difficult both to measure and to manage. An education index provides a useful framework for measurement, but the challenges of education—and the issues that are at stake—are clearly highlighted by the example of India. While it is achieving definite improvement now, it is starting from a significantly lower base and will be hard pressed to catch up with other regions in the world. Fortunately, history provides us with encouraging examples of other societies—for example, Thailand and China—that have managed to meet this challenge and, as a result, are benefiting economically and socially.

This chapter has highlighted the two-way connections between education and demographic change. In the next chapter, this is taken a stage further. If demography begins to affect a society through education, then it continues to have an impact through the labour force. This is another two-way relationship (with the size and nature of the workforce influencing demography and vice versa), which will be the focus for the next chapter.

Chapter 5

The Evolving
Labour Force

A t a national level, the trends in the size and capability (which is a
function of education) of the labour force significantly determine the health of the economy and how it will grow. This in
turn impacts wages, household incomes, and expenditures. Therefore, it
is important to understand the drivers behind the size and productivity
of the labour force and their implications for the future size and capability of the labour force. It is also important to have an appreciation of
how the very nature of those drivers is changing and in particular, how
an extended working age is changing the perceived ability of many
countries to develop their economy.

This chapter should also impact on perceptions about the future
course of some economies. A trick question is a useful starting point.
Country A has a labour force which will shrink in absolute number of
workers by 18 percent over the next two decades. Country B has a

labour force that is 10 times more productive than that of Country A and whose number of workers will increase by 13 percent over the next two decades. Which one should be promoted as a good investment environment? Which countries are they? Read on!

Factors Influencing the Size and Value of the Labour Force

The size of the labour force, and how that will change, is driven by the age profile of the population which determines the number of persons of working age, and then their propensity to be employed, which itself is a function of education (capability) and social norms (such as acceptance of the involvement of women in the workplace).

The Working Age Population

The most important determinant of the size of the labour force is the number of people of working age, typically defined as being 15 years to 64 years of age. However, this assumption needs to be modified to reflect the longer lifespan that is now evident in the affluent regions of the world, and the consequent changes that are occurring in propensity to work at older ages.

In many of the more affluent countries, including North America, most of Western Europe, and most of Affluent Asia, the improved quality of nutrition combined with good and improving levels of health care have led to people living significantly longer, and they are fitter and healthier for much of that time. In Japan, life expectancy has risen to 84 years—double that of the world's least-developed nations. In many other developed nations, life expectancy is in the late 70s and early 80s.

This has two significant implications for older people's desire and need to find work. First, there are new, personal economic imperatives. If an individual retires at age 65 and lives in a country with a long life expectancy, they will need to fund on average an additional 15 more years of life. Even as recently as 20 or 30 years ago, this was not the case. The existing pension and savings funds in these countries are insufficient to provide for everyone to live a leisurely, retired life for an extended period longer than originally intended—about 10 years.

In many countries, pensions and savings have simply failed to keep up with changing economic realities, personal circumstances, and lifestyles. As a result, there is an increasing pressure on individuals to work longer.

Also, these people who are living longer are still physically active and intellectually able. Turning 65 does not switch off the brain, and the prospect of being stuck at home or playing golf every day is unappealing to many 65-year-olds. The point of view held by many governments is that this wish to remain in the workforce is desirable, as it reduces the pension liability on public funds. Most Western European economies are changing legislation right now to reflect this change in attitude as well as economic realities, and in some Western European countries, the actual (rather than legal) average retirement age of males is already over 65 years.

While this might seem like a fairly minor change at a national economic level, the reality is that, in these older countries, it increases the pool of individuals available to be in the labour force more significantly than many realise. Japan is an interesting example, particularly as many commentators focus on its potential inability to provide for its ageing population. If working age was *not* expanded from 15 to 64 to 15 to 70 by 2032, then the working-age population would only compose 59 percent of the Japanese people in 2032, limiting its productive capacity. Adding an extra five years to working life increases the working-age population from 63 percent of the total population in 2012 to 67 percent in 2032. In absolute terms, this change would add another 8.1 million people to the size of the working-age population. This extension of working-age definition expands the potential pool of workers in North America, Western Europe, and Affluent Asia. The other regions at this stage do not have a life expectancy that would allow such a general social adjustment to be made.

Figure 5.1 shows the projected change in the number of persons that are of working age in each of the regions between 2012 and 2032,

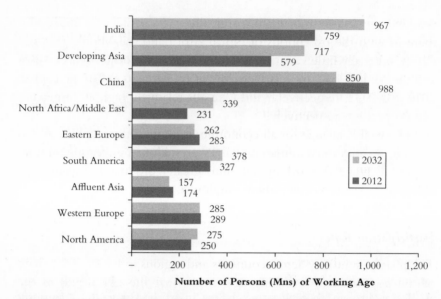

Figure 5.1   Number of Persons (Millions) of Working Age in 2012 and 2032
Source: Global Demographics Ltd.

taking into account the longer working-age range in the older and more affluent countries. In total, the number of people of working age in the 74 countries covered in this book is projected to increase from 3.9 billion in 2012 to 4.2 billion by 2032. This means there will be a net increase of 349 million persons of working age over the next 20 years, a growth rate of 0.5 percent per annum. Interestingly, Figure 5.1 highlights significant differences in trends across the regions. In North America it increases, in Western Europe it is stable, and in Affluent Asia it declines. South America, North Africa and the Middle East, and Developing Asia, all having younger populations, are projected to experience a significant increase in the potential pool of labour. So too is India for the same reasons—but what a contrast India is to China. Whereas India is projected to have an additional 207 million persons of working age in the next two decades, China will have 138 million less.

It is worth noting that overall for the countries covered in this book, in 2012 an estimated 68 percent of the populations are of working age and this decreases marginally to 66 percent by 2032. Also there is, with the exceptions of North Africa and the Middle East and China, relatively little variation around this global average. North Africa and the Middle East are relatively low at 61 percent and 62 percent in 2012 and 2032, respectively, and China is relatively high at 73 percent and 66 percent, respectively.

The vital challenge for all economies is how far they will be able to convert this additional human capital, as a result of an increasing number of persons being of working age, into greater productive capability—that is getting and keeping them employed.

Participation Rates

The relative similarity across countries and regions in terms of the share of the population of working age means that the key driver of the economies is not what proportion of their populations are of working age but, rather, their ability to engage them in employment. That is the propensity of working-age persons to be employed. The reader is reminded that this is very different from unemployment rates. Unemployment rate is the proportion of persons *seeking* work who cannot find work. However, not all persons of working age are seeking work. So the employment rate is the proportion of people of working age who are seeking *and* who found work. It is necessary to use this approach as data is not generally available on the proportion of those of working age who are seeking work. It is also a more robust measure and therefore more appropriate for international comparisons.

The percentage of working age that is employed is called the *participation rate* and it is a function of many factors, including how long people spend in education (the better the education system, the later their entry into the labour force), attitudes toward female participation, and, finally, the availability of work (which effectively determines the unemployment rate).

The participation rate can vary as a result of multiple external factors. However, an analysis of the last two decades suggests that participation rates vary around a clear trend line for each country and region, and that trend is what is used for the forecast in 2032.

Figure 5.2 Participation Rates by Gender in 2012
Source: Global Demographics Ltd.

When looking at the workforce participation rate, it is important to break the analysis down by gender, as there are significant differences between them. Figure 5.2 shows the participation rate of men and women for each region in 2012. In most countries, the male participation rate is close to the overall average of 77 percent, meaning that slightly more than three out of every four males of working age are participating in the labour force—that is, employed. In Eastern Europe this figure is 67 percent; in Developing Asia it is 81 percent and China at 83 percent. Contrast this with female participation rates. By a substantial margin China has the highest female participation rates at 71 percent. The next highest region is North America at 63 percent. This is followed by Affluent Asia, with 58 percent, and Western Europe with 57 percent. Perhaps, unsurprisingly, female participation rates are by far the lowest in North Africa and the Middle East at around 30 percent for a variety of reasons, notably social and cultural, but also gender differences in educational opportunities. It is also worth noting that in Developing Asia there is a significant dichotomy. In Thailand and

Vietnam the female participation rate is over 70 percent whereas in Indonesia, Malaysia, and the Philippines it is around 47 percent and for the others it is below 30 percent.

As the size of the total labour force is substantially determined by the proportion of the working-age population that is employed, these percentages are crucial and what is particularly significant is how the trend will develop over the next two decades. For men, the general consensus is that the participation rate will remain relatively steady, but with a marginal decline in some countries where the access to education is improving and thus delays their entry into the workforce. This contrasts with the female participation rate, which is expected to increase marginally as more women gain equal access to education and as social attitudes change towards women working. However, it is interesting to note that the trend in female participation between 2000 and 2010 provides no evidence of significant change, even in countries where there is no difference in educational outcomes by gender. So only a gradual increase can be planned for.

The exception to this is Japan. There is a significant change in behaviour happening there, and female participation rates have increased significantly over the last decade, reflecting a change in attitudes to female participation (there has been relatively little difference in gender education profile for some decades so that is not the cause of the change). This trend of the older working age empty nester female entering/returning to the workforce is expected to continue for the next two decades and has a significant impact on the size of Japan's total labour force.

Finally, with respect of participation rates, it is important to note the situation in China. With male participation rate of 83 percent and a female rate of 71 percent it can be stated that China is operating at full capacity in terms of its labour resources. While it might be overstating the participation rate in the rural areas, the point remains that it is unlikely that any society can expect a higher proportion of working-age adults to be employed. Consequently, China has no spare labour resource and the trend in working age population is critical to determining the future size of its total labour force, and that (working-age population) is projected to decline from 988 million in 2012 to a projected 850 million in 2032.

Implications for Existing Labour Force Size

The size of the labour force in 2012 can be estimated by applying the participation rates to the working-age population. The resulting estimated employed population is considered to be quite reliable and provide a good basis for economic planning.

In 2012, the global workforce is around 2.54 billion people. Understanding where these people are located, however, reveals an interesting picture that is highlighted in Figure 5.3.

Given its large population, it is not surprising that China accounts for 30 percent of the global workforce. In contrast, India, with almost the same total population as China, accounts for just 17 percent of the global total. Its total labour force is little more than half the size of China's. This is due to differences in age profile of the population and in female participation rates. In terms of working age female population, for India only 39 percent are employed whereas for China it is 71 percent. The other factor influencing the difference is age profile. India is much younger, as explained in Chapter 1, and as a result has a lower proportion of its population falling within working age band. That is

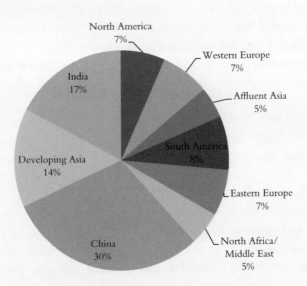

Figure 5.3 Regional Share of Global Workforce in 2012
Source: Global Demographics Ltd.

64 percent. For China the working-age population as a proportion of total population is 73 percent.

Finally, in respect of the 2012 scenario, slightly under two out of three workers in the world are located in Asia (India, China, Developing Asia, and Affluent Asia).

The Future Labour Force

The total global labour force is expected to increase by 176 million people by 2032. However, there are significant differences in the trend and absolute amount of change by region.

Figure 5.4 shows the absolute size of the labour force in each region in 2012 and as projected for 2032, taking into account the changing size of the working-age population and the likely (marginal) trends in propensity to be employed. There are some clear patterns in the changes expected. Basically, the young regions are all expected to have significant (greater than 18 percent) increases in the size of their labour forces over the next two decades. This applies to Developing Asia, India, North

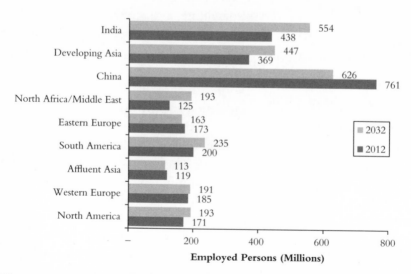

Figure 5.4   Total Employed Persons (Millions) in 2012 and 2032
Source: Global Demographics Ltd.

Keep in mind the fact that the costs of manufacturing will change dramatically as a result of robotics, 3D printing, and other innovations that will have a profound effect during the next 20 years. This will have a major impact on the demand for low-skilled labour. It's worth remembering that the IBM PC was introduced in 1984—just 28 years ago. At that time nobody had a desktop computer—today, most people do—and this has displaced many low-end jobs. Robotics is now probably at the equivalent of 1990 in terms of computer adoption.

Africa and the Middle East, and finally South America. Not surprisingly, at 54 percent, the largest increase will be in the North Africa and Middle East region. Even middle-aged South America is expected to have an 18 percent increase in total labour force. This does raise the question as to whether there will be enough jobs for all these young people entering working age and seeking work. The trend in propensity to be employed assumes that employment opportunities grow in line with it. Obviously under this scenario (supply of labour potentially exceeding demand), that could be tested. At the very least, it will place continuing downward pressure on wages in these areas as there is a real probability that supply will exceed demand—especially if the export markets of these regions are moderating their demand for physical goods and moving more to experience expenditure, as discussed in Chapter 8.

In contrast, the older regions of the world are projected to have quite stable total labour force size with the exception of North America which, with its younger population and growth through migration, is expected to increase its total labour force by 13 percent in absolute size over the next 20 years. This contrasts significantly with the scenario in China.

China's labour force will inevitably shrink, and quite rapidly. Given the country's ageing population and the resulting decline in the number of people of working age, and that it is already fully utilising its working-age adult population, it is expected that the number of employed people in China will decline from 761 million people to 626 million by 2032.

That is a reduction of 135 million people in 20 years from China's labour force. It is a decline in size of 18 percent and is an interesting juxtaposition against North America, whose labour force is projected to grow by 13 percent over the same period.

This decline in the absolute size of the labour force has interesting implications for China's total economic growth and where it might be in future. There can be few, if any, societies in human history that have ever experienced such a rapid decline in the number of workers as China inevitably will. It is inevitable because the two parameters driving it are the number of persons of working age and propensity to work. The first of these is closely defined as most of the people that will be working age by 2032 are already alive today so it can be forecast with some accuracy. The only possible variable is propensity of those people to be employed. In this respect, China already has one of the highest rates for propensity to be employed in the world and effectively has no spare capacity. It is unlikely the propensity to be employed can be higher than its present level. Therefore, there is the certainty of the decline in the total size of China's workforce.

This does have significant implications for economic forecasts for China. For the last two decades up to 2010, China has been adding approximately six million workers every year to its labour force which, combined with increased productivity per worker and massive fixed capital investment, has helped China enjoy a period of rapid growth in total GDP. However, in future, the Chinese labour force will begin to decline at an average rate of 6.7 million workers per annum over the next two decades.

For China's total economy to continue to grow at the rate it has for the last 10 years, China's productivity per worker will have to increase significantly. As we saw earlier in Chapter 4, China's overall standard of education is approaching the point where productivity per worker could improve significantly. However, the reader is reminded that growth in total GDP is less important in a country that has a declining (or even flat) total population. What is more important is that the per capita GDP is growing—and in China's case the prognosis is good as a result of improving education of the workforce. So perhaps one can be skeptical about the very optimistic headline growth rate forecasts of some for total

GDP but, nonetheless, remain positive about the overall well-being of China's population.

There is one other vital question to consider: That is the trend in labour forces in the countries which are able to extend working age, as discussed in the previous section of this chapter. Before looking at a specific example in respect of this, it is worth noting the headline statistics. For North America, the total employed labour force will grow by 13 percent in absolute size in the next two decades, aided by an extra 25 million persons being working age and with a slight increase in the propensity of these persons to be employed (although the 65- to 69-year-olds are at 50 percent of the average rate for propensity to be employed). The same factors mean that in Western Europe the labour force is projected to grow by 3 percent. In the case of Affluent Asia, it is projected to decline by 5 percent over the next 20 years—this decline taking place particularly in South Korea and Taiwan and, to a much lesser extent, in Japan.

Japan is an interesting specific example in this respect, as many commentators have been saying that its economic future is dismal because the aging population will inevitably result in a declining workforce relative to the overall population. However, there are two factors at play which give a different outcome from the obvious one. The first is the extension of working age, which is not really a matter of choice but rather economic necessity, as the average individual otherwise faces the prospect of funding a 20-year retirement. The implication of this is that by 2032, there are an additional 7.5 million persons of working age—an 11 percent increase on what would have otherwise been the case.

In addition, there is in Japan the unusual situation of increasing participation rates. Female participation rate is expected to increase from 60 percent of the female working age population to 68 percent. In part, this is the result of older, well-educated women (aged 40 years plus) entering the labour force for the first time as a result of the unusual combination of capability (Japanese females have been as well educated as males for some considerable time now) and changing acceptance of female participation. Taken together, these factors suggest that Japan's total labour force will decline from its current level of 62.8 million people to 59 million in the years to 2032, contrary to the traditional case, which would have it declining to 56 million by 2032. Basically, while the total population will decline by 9 percent, the portion of the population that is working will increase, and the total labour force will decline only 6 percent in size. So, rather than being a weakened economy, it is actually strengthening its position—high productive capacity and very low dependency ratios—which (as discussed next in this chapter) mean greater capability to both save and engage in discretionary spending.

Twin Challenges: Dependency and Productivity

The number and proportion of the population that is employed are, however, just the first step in understanding changes in the labour force. The number of employed persons has to be examined in two further aspects. The first is *dependency rates*, how many people are supported by each worker, as that directly impacts consumption patterns. The second is *productivity trends*, as this determines the value of the worker and ultimately the economic value of the society and its ability to consume.

Understanding Dependency Ratios   Having analysed the number of employed people in the population and the implications for size of the labour force, we can now return to the number of dependent people who are relying on each worker, a figure known as the *dependency ratio*. As we saw in Chapter 3, this vital economic statistic determines each household's ability both to save and to consume. Clearly, if fewer people are dependent on each worker, then the average household is effectively richer in that it has a higher income per capita. Figure 5.5 shows the dependency ratios for each region and how this is expected to change between 2012 and 2032.

The first point to note is that there are considerable differences between each of the regions. In 2012, China, at 0.77, has by far the lowest dependency ratio. North Africa and the Middle East have the highest ratio, at 2.04. To appreciate the consequences of this, consider a worker in each region earning $3000 per annum. In China, that equates to $1,694 per person (one worker and 0.71 dependents). In the Middle East or North Africa, the same earnings provide $983 per person (US$3,000 divided by 3.04, being one worker and 2.04 dependents).

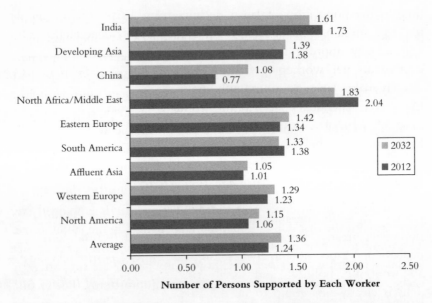

Figure 5.5 Number of Persons Supported by Each Worker
Source: Global Demographics Ltd.

The forecast reveals diverse trends in the dependency ratio in the years to 2032. In China, with a declining working age population, the dependency ratio rises to 1.08. In comparison, India's dependency ratio falls from 1.73 to 1.61 and it is also expected to fall in North Africa and the Middle East, from 2.04 to 1.83, and in South America from 1.38 to 1.33. As in these cases, the proportion of the population that is working age increases and with that (hopefully) employment. Generally, though, for most of the 74 countries considered in our analysis, the dependency ratio is projected to increase marginally.

Once again, the situation in Japan provides an interesting and unexpected trend—one that also extends to many of the countries in West Europe and Affluent Asia. As we mentioned earlier, greater life expectancy, combined with the increasing desire and ability of the 65- to 69-year-old age group to work and with increasing female participation in the workforce, means that the total Japanese labour force is expected to decline by 6 percent from its present level of 63 million people to 59 million over the next 20 years. This will happen at the same time as the population of Japan declines from 127.4 million people to 115.7 million. The obvious result is that Japan's dependency ratio will actually improve from 1.03 to 0.96 dependents per worker—a figure which actually makes Japan a country with one of the lowest dependency ratios in the world in 2032. Crucially, this means that Japan hardly needs to be concerned about the economy's ability to provide for the aged population.

The popular misconception is that Japan's low birth rate and ageing population will greatly worsen the country's dependency ratio, potentially resulting in an economic, political, and social crisis. This is clearly not going to be the case. Commentators have failed to take into account the realities of Japanese life, in particular an increased lifespan, extended work life and greater use of robotics, and the implications of all of these issues for Japan's dependency ratio. Finally, it is worth noting that the trend for dependency ratios to reduce is also accompanied by the trend for household incomes to increase, as discussed in the next chapter. Combining the two means that, in Japan, overall per capita income, and consequently people's standards of living, can be expected to improve.

> *The trend for dependency ratios to reduce in Japan is also accompanied by the trend for household incomes to increase. Combining the two means that overall per capita income, and consequently people's standards of living, can be expected to improve in that country.*

And Productivity per Worker   Finally, to understand the global labour force, we need to examine the cost effectiveness of employing someone in each country, and how this might develop in the years to 2032. Given that we know average household income and the average number of workers per household, we can determine the average wage per worker. Similarly, because we also know total GDP and the total number of workers, we can determine, with a high degree of reliability, the gross productivity per worker. While a crude measure of productivity, it is reliable and not subject to fudging. Following this analysis through, by dividing GDP per worker by the average wage we can then

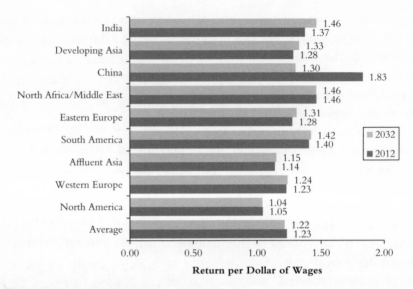

Figure 5.6   Return per Dollar of Wages
Source: Global Demographics Ltd.

estimate the return to the economy (and, on average, to the employer) on every dollar of wage paid to a worker. Figure 5.6 highlights the situation in 2012 and 2032.

Looking at the 2012 data, the obvious issue is the high returns generated in China. For every $1 in Chinese wages there is an output of $1.83. The next highest return on wages is in North Africa and the Middle East, at $1.46 of output per $1 paid followed by South America at $1.40. These numbers explain why China attracted so much investment in manufacturing. This situation also reflects the fact that China's salaries are quite low as a proportion of total economic activity. We'll return to this issue when we consider household incomes in Chapter 6, but for now it is enough to know that the private consumption component of GDP, which is a reliable measure of total household expenditure (and incomes), is just 33 percent of GDP in China in 2010 (latest published), whereas for most countries it is over 60 percent and for many it is over 70 percent.

The situation in which Chinese workers receive a disproportionately small share of the total economic activity matters for two important reasons. Firstly, relative to the size of GDP, the proportion of the total economy in China that is available for the consumer is significantly lower than in most other countries As such, the GDP is not a good indicator of the value of the consumer market in a country, and particularly China. Secondly, this situation will inevitably change. As we have already seen, the number of employed persons in China will inevitably decline. Given the already high participation rates of the Chinese labour force, there is little spare capacity, putting an inflationary pressure on wages. It is already evident along China's eastern seaboard that incomes are rising—and factories in central and western China are moving in the same direction. Furthermore, it is the Chinese government's stated intention to increase the share of the economy that goes back to the worker by steadily increasing the minimum wage paid in the state-owned enterprises (who are the largest employers in China), which, in turn, impacts on the cost of labour in the private sector.

As a result of these changes, it is projected that the return per dollar wage in China, in real terms, will decline by 2032 to $1.30 for every $1.00 spent on wages. This is a significant economic development, as there are many other countries already near or above that level of return and will close the gap further by 2032. For example, in 2012 the return per dollar spent in Indonesia is US$1.45, in Brazil $1.57, Azerbaijan $1.9, Czech Republic $1.56, Romania $1.73 and Malaysia $1.63—and they are all likely to improve on this dimension.

This matters because China will become a less-attractive destination for investment in manufacturing and increasingly important as an export market for other countries as the domestic market grows as a result of higher wages. In addition, with some countries becoming increasingly competitive as areas in which to invest, this will attract production out of China. While, on the one hand it will constrain China's total GDP growth (negative trade balance being one factor), it will also impact on the cost of labour in the

> *As a result of these changes, it is projected that the return per dollar wage in China, in real terms, will decline by 2032 to $1.30 for every $1.00 spent on wages. This is a significant economic development, as there are many other countries already near or above that level of return and will close the gap further by 2032.*

other developing countries (e.g., Indonesia) as the demand for labour there will increase and, with that, the potential for real wage increases and increased consumer demand.

Strategic Implications

First it is important to understand that, while the global labour force will continue to grow in size, albeit now relatively slowly, technology will have an enormous impact on the demand for that labour and where production is located. We will see many important changes over the next 20 years, including the continuing development and application of robotics and 3D printing, as well as a quickening pace of innovation. Taken together, these developments will profoundly affect the costs of manufacturing and will decrease the demand for low-skilled labour and increase the capability of older, more experienced labour. It could well foretell the shift of manufacturing back to the older, better-educated economies with potentially disastrous implications for the developing world. India's demographic dividend could well become its demographic liability—thus, the importance of the ability of countries like India to raise their education standard rapidly. Otherwise, robots will take the work that would have been done by the unskilled labour forces.

The second major strategic issue to flow from this analysis is that China's labour costs will inevitably increase simply as result of shortage of supply. It will, however, be further encouraged by the government's stated intention to rebalance the economy to consumption and to do that by encouraging the increase of real wages. This will impact China's competitiveness and will probably result in the movement of lower skilled (and perhaps even higher skilled) labour demand to other countries such as Indonesia and some Eastern European and South American countries, where the cost is now competitive with that of China. So expect some movement of manufacture and also perhaps more rapid growth of these economies as the cost of their labour is bid up by increased demand for it. Eastern Europe, with its closer access to the large Western European market, as well as its own markets (in terms of total consumer spending it matches China), is expected to benefit significantly from this change in relative cost efficiencies given its logistic advantages as well. It could not compete when China is over $1.77 return per $1 wage, but it can at $1.30. The same argument can be advanced in terms of South America (and particularly Mexico), given its access to the large North American consumer market.

Finally, reconsider the older countries, particularly Japan. Their labour forces are not shrinking relative to the total population and their education standard and productivity per worker are very high. These economies are not under threat and actually have growth potential—the extreme case being North America. The expectation that they will be overtaken by the large population but low income economies does not bear scrutiny.

Summary

With the exceptions of Affluent Asia, Eastern Europe, and China, the total employed labour force of the regions will grow over the next two decades—driven by a combination of an increased proportion of the population being of working age and increased propensity to be employed. The major anomaly will be China. Its capacity for growth is, in one important respect, going to be constrained: The number of persons of working age has gone into decline and, as the country is already at full employment (it has very high participation rates already), this means the total labour force will also decline. China's situation contrasts with many other countries, such as India, that are younger (in terms of population age) and poorer. For these countries, an ability to increase female participation in the labour force provides a major opportunity to stimulate economic growth. To date, these countries have not shown much inclination to increase female participation and the forecasts here assume only slow increases. However, if these countries could change this attitude more quickly than has been apparent, whole countries and regions could be transformed economically—from India to the Middle East and North Africa—assuming there is work for them.

A major factor leading to the growth of the labour force (or lack of decline in the case of specific countries such as Japan) is the changing practice in terms of what is retirement age. It is extending beyond

60 years and by 2032 it will not be unusual for a person aged 69 to be in employment. This change in attitude is a function of improved life span (a function of health) and is still largely constrained to the affluent regions of the world. China and much of Developing Asia, for example, have not reached the same life expectancy yet (for adults aged 50 today). They will start to catch up in the subsequent two decades.

Finally, to answer the question at the start of this chapter, Country A is China and Country B is the USA, yet how often is the USA described as the investment opportunity of the next decade, and how often is that title given to China?

In the next chapter we continue with the theme of economic development and spending—so vital for individuals, businesses, societies, and the future—and ask: Where in the world is the money?

Chapter 6

Where in the World Is the Money?

This chapter explains the relative importance of different regions and countries in terms of total earned household income, and shows how just three regions account for 71 percent of total global incomes and 69 percent of household spending (and they may not be the three places you think they are). It also gives a more balanced and rigorous view of the origins of—and trends in—future consumption. The next chapter will look at the distribution of households by income and where the affluent and poor are. The focus in this chapter is on total earned income.

Elephants in the Room

Discussions about money and wealth are so sensitive and significant that they can give rise to concerns—valid or otherwise—about any use of data on this subject. These concerns can undermine any discussion on these issues and so they need to be resolved. In fact, there are several elephants in the room, each of which is discussed subsequently.

How Reliable Are the Available Data?

There is, invariably, debate about what the average (or median) household income is in a country. Individuals form impressions from the society they see, and there is always debate about the existence and size of an undeclared economy. This latter point being particularly true for income figures derived from a consumer survey where respondents may well understate income for a variety of reasons. However, there is actually a reliable sanity check available for a country's average household income. The calculation works like this. First, the household component of private consumption expenditure component of a country's GDP is the total expenditure of all households in that country plus charities (although generally the latter is generally not significant as a proportion). Dividing this figure by the (generally well known) total number of households provides a reliable measure of the average household's expenditure per annum. What is more, as it is based on the expenditure side of GDP calculations, it is obtained from retail sales, warehouse shipments, and so on, it picks up all expenditure, even if the associated income has not been properly declared in tax returns and income surveys. To disagree with this average household *expenditure* figure you have to either change the total number of households or total GDP, both of which tend to be quite reliable measures. As such, this derived average expenditure per household gives a good reference point from which to estimate average pre- and posttax household incomes given the relationship between expenditure and after tax income in each country's household income and expenditure survey or its equivalent. In most countries this is usually completed each year by the census department. The pretax income can then be determined by application of the tax tables for the individual countries.

Of course, like all research on sensitive issues such as income, these household income and expenditure studies being used to determine the relation between expenditure and savings may contain error (both respondent errors and nonresponse errors). Even so, they do provide the best available measure of the distribution of households by expenditure and income and, more importantly, a good measure of the proportion of income that is spent by income level.

This process for calculating household incomes has been used by Global Demographics Ltd. for the 74 countries covered in this book. While it will include some error in estimation, it is still, we believe, a largely good estimate of average household's income and expenditure, and one with a reliable and consistent underpinning for each country. So the relative income level for each country can be defended with some confidence.

Usefulness of GDP for Evaluating the Potential of the Consumer Market of One Country Relative to Another

This leads us to the second elephant in the room: the use of GDP as a measure of individual prosperity in a country and the relative value or attractiveness of the consumer market. Clearly, GDP is important as it encompasses the whole economy, not just the consumer proportion. However, the real issue, from the point of view of consumer products and services, is the proportion of the total economy that ends up in the consumers' hands for them to spend. As mentioned previously, this is the private consumption expenditure component of GDP and the share of total GDP that it represents varies significantly between countries. For example, much was made of the fact that China's total GDP now exceeds that of Japan. Given the current exchange rates, it is a reality and is important but, if your concern is with the opportunity for a consumer product or service, it would be erroneous to consider today's Chinese market as being as important as that of Japan. The reason for this is that in 2011 Private Consumption Expenditure component of the total GDP in Japan is 60 percent of total GDP, whereas in China it is 33 percent. The impact of this is shown in Figure 6.1.

Trying to compare consumer spending levels between countries by using total GDP is misleading as the consumer share of the economy varies by country—from a low of 33 percent to a high of 86 percent.

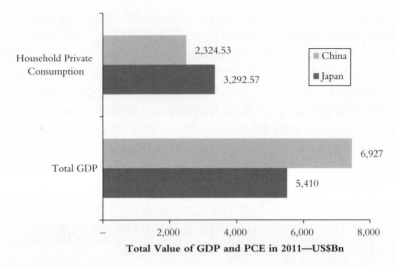

Figure 6.1 Relative Consumer Markets—China and Japan (2011)
Source: Global Demographics Ltd.

> *In 2012, China's estimated total GDP is 28 percent greater than Japan's; however, the private consumption expenditure component, which is effectively the amount of money that the people in each country have to spend, is 42 percent greater in Japan than it is in China.*

Even allowing for the fact that the US dollar value of each of these two economies is a function of whatever exchange rate is being used, the picture here makes the point. In 2011, China's total GDP was 28 percent greater than that of Japan; however the private consumption expenditure component, which is effectively the amount of money that people in each country had to spend, was 42 percent greater in Japan than in China. So from a consumer market point of view the Japanese consumer market is significantly the more important of the two.

Crucially, the private expenditure component's share of GDP varies across all regions and countries. China has the second lowest private consumption expenditure (PCE) percentage of the 74 countries included in this study, the simple (unweighted) average for all countries is 59 percent and, for the more affluent world, it averages 55 percent. For this reason, when comparing between countries/regions in terms of potential of the *consumer* market, it is best to look at the PCE component of the economy rather than GDP.

Finally, in respect to this, it is important the reader notes that the government of China has a specific economic object of increasing the proportion of the GDP ending up in the consumer's hands and this will lead to faster growth of wages and household incomes than that of the GDP as a whole. This is incorporated in the forecasts of household incomes in subsequent sections of this and the next chapter. In other countries the trend in the share of GDP that is Private Consumption Expenditure reflects trends in supply of labour and education.

What Is the Best Way to Compare Expenditure among Countries?

There is a third and final elephant in the room that we also need to recognise (it's clearly a large room), and that is misunderstandings in terms of purchasing power parity (PPP). In this book all financial data are reported in US dollars, using the average exchange rate to USD for 2011 and 2010 real local currency values (that is, all inflation is removed from historic data and all forecasts are in real terms making no assumptions about inflation). We are not inclined to adjust these values to a PPP index for two reasons. First, the index itself is subject to wide criticism regarding its weighting. Second, when evaluating a market there is a fixed amount of money that people have to spend, and multiplying it by some index value is misleading, making some markets look disproportionately more valuable.

To explain, compare China and the USA in terms of beverage expenditure. In China, an individual will get 1.50 (current PPP index value) more beverage *volume* for US$10 than a person in the USA (the USA is the reference point). That is because it is possible to produce beverages cheaper in China than in America. However, what it also means is that an American brand wanting to sell in China has to drop its price to 66 percent of its USA price to be price competitive—with implications for total market value for that brand and profit achieved. Purchasing power parity *does not mean* that a person in China has 1.5 times more money to spend on beverages than a person in the USA; it simply means that on average things are 33 percent cheaper in China.

So, Where Is the Money?

The clearest way to understand this is by looking at the two pie charts in Figure 6.2. The left-hand one (A) shows the distribution of the world's population by region in 2012. The right-hand pie chart (B) shows the proportion of total earned household income accounted for by each region in the same year. Total earned household income is the average household income of a country multiplied by the number of households in the same country (summed for the region). The differences between the two charts in terms of the relative share accounted for by each region are considerable and might even be surprising to some in terms of the relative importance of specific regions.

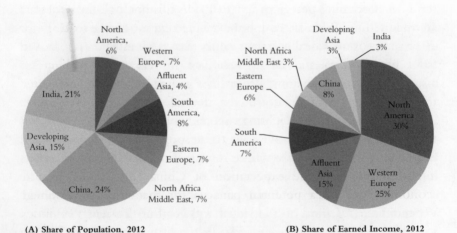

(A) Share of Population, 2012   (B) Share of Earned Income, 2012

Figure 6.2 Regional Share of Population (A) and Total Earned Income 2012 (B)
Source: Global Demographics Ltd.

Figure 6.2 (A) shows regional share of total population in the countries covered by this study, as shown in Chapter 1. It reminds us that China and India account for nearly half the world's population, with Developing Asia, the Middle East, North Africa, South America, and Eastern Europe having a further 30 percent, leaving just under 18 percent of the world's population living in North America, Western Europe, and Affluent Asia. The reader is, however, reminded that the countries included in this chart account for 79 percent of the world's population. As such, these percentages are overstated from a truly global point of view.

Figure 6.2 (B) shows the share of total earned household income accounted for by each region. The total earned incomes in North America and Western Europe and Affluent Asia currently (2012) are estimated to account for 70.5 percent of total consumer spending in the world, while they contain 18 percent of the world's population. This contrasts with China, which accounts for 24 percent of the world's population and 8 percent of the world's consumer expenditure, and India, with 21 percent of the world's population and just 3 percent of the world's consumer expenditure. This reflects very significant differences in average household income, an issue we will explain later in this chapter.

The important strategic point that flows from this 2012 situation is, while China and India may be showing high headline growth rates in absolute terms, the important consumer markets in 2012 are the older affluent markets. The sustainability of a company will depend on its ability to achieve and maintain a strong position in the older affluent markets, which account for most of the consumer spending. Success in the smaller, but fast growing, consumer markets of India and China is clearly attractive (and to be sought) but is not an end in itself and is not necessarily where resources should be concentrated. It also shows how the expectation of China and India's growth economies will be a potential panacea for the currently troubled Western European and (to a lesser extent) North American economies is perhaps without good foundation. It is a little unrealistic to expect 11 percent of the global consumer market to provide a substitute for 71 percent of the global consumer market.

Relative Average Household Incomes per Capita in 2012

Obviously, the difference between the two pie charts in Figure 6.2 is a reflection of the difference in household income per capita between countries and, therefore, regions. This is shown in Figure 6.3, which depicts how significantly, in absolute terms, household income per capita varies across the world. The affluent regions per capita incomes are greater than the poor regions by a factor of 10, which is why 18 percent of the world's population accounts for 71 percent of the world's total earned income and, ultimately, consumption power. Furthermore, as shown later in this chapter, it is naive to assume this difference will erode over the next two decades. Even though the poorer regions have faster growth rates (which to a considerable extent is a function of the lower base on which the growth is calculated), the affluent will also be growing and have a significant lead that will not be closed in a decade or two.

Per capita incomes are used here to compare between countries and regions because there are significant differences in household size that

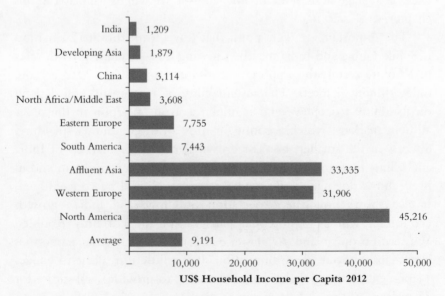

Figure 6.3   Relative Household Income per Capita in 2012 (US$ per Annum)
Source: Global Demographics Ltd.

impact the relative funds available per person, which is a better basis of comparison of spending power. But while per capita income is a better measure of the spending power of individuals, the reality is that most income data are measured and reported on a per household basis, so it is generally better to examine the current state of incomes across the regions on a per household basis.

Figure 6.4 shows the average and median (midpoint) household income before tax and savings for each region. When it comes to household income, the world can be divided into three distinct groups: those regions where average annual income is more than US$60,000 per annum, those where it is between US$10,000 and

It is important to keep in mind the fact that there are major differences between the average household sizes in different countries, meaning that similar household income levels may support very different numbers of people.

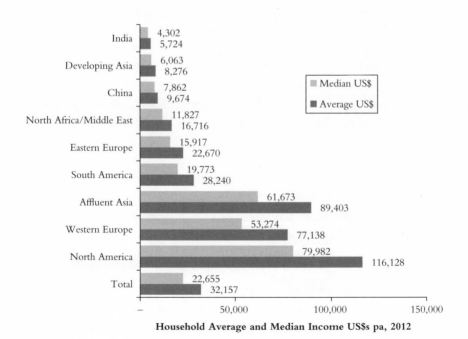

Household Average and Median Income US$s pa, 2012

Figure 6.4   Household Average and Median Household Incomes, 2012
Source: Global Demographics Ltd.

US$30,000 and those with average incomes under US$10,000 per annum. Clearly, there are major differences in the consumption power of households in each of these three groups, especially as, typically, when household income goes down, the number of persons per household increases—thereby lowering per capita incomes further as explained previously.

Where Will the Money Be in the Future?

This next section looks at the projected changes in relative incomes across the regions over the next 20 years. In order to do this, we must first examine the assumptions used to forecast growth in GDPs and share of that which goes to private consumption, as these two variables effectively determine the absolute level of household incomes.

Understanding the Assumptions

Before giving the forecast of how incomes and spending will change over the next 20 years, we must first explain our assumptions for economic growth and our method for forecasting GDP (the total output of all workers in an economy) and the share of it that goes to the private sector (the households) and, ultimately, household incomes.

There are two key components to these GDP and household income forecasts: the number of employed people (overall and per household) and the productivity (or output) of each employed person. The number of employed people is the number of people of working age multiplied by their propensity to be employed, as discussed in Chapter 5. The second component is productivity per worker, which is a function of education and investment. Using our historic data on the education index from Chapter 4 and GDP per worker, we can determine the historic relationship of education to productivity per worker and, given the projected future value of the education index, estimate the projected future productivity of each worker. We then multiply the projected number of workers by their projected productivity to produce an estimate of total GDP for each country.

Finally, we use the trend in share of total GDP that is private consumption expenditure (relative to the supply and education of labour) to determine what proportion of the economy ends up in the hands of the households. This divided by the number of households gives a very reliable measure of the average household expenditure. As it is based on the expenditure side of GDP, it includes all expenditure irrespective of whether or not the income has been declared for tax purposes. By using the results of the Household Income and Expenditure Survey for each country, it is then possible to determine the gross (pretax) income needed for that level of spend and also tax and, by implication, savings. The same survey gives a measure of the distribution of households by income and spending pattern by income level. There will be some error in these estimates as they are using survey rather than census data but they are anchored on the known average expenditure per household so will be sensible and defensible overall.

Overall, our forecasts of GDP and household income are much more conservative than those widely published in the financial press and by the IMF and can, perhaps, be seen as a worst-case scenario. So what is the result of this analysis?

The Economies of the Future

Table 6.1 (A) shows the present and projected total real GDP in US$ billions for each region. The reader is reminded that these values are expressed in 2010 values and exclude inflation. Focusing first on the real, total GDP, it is clear that China, India, and Developing Asia will have by far the highest economic growth rates for the next 20 years. The demographic model indicates average growth rates of 3.3 percent per annum for China, 5.17 percent for India and 3.54 percent for Developing Asia. China will achieve this growth by increasing the productivity of its workforce, on the basis of its improving and relatively high education standards. This will offset the 16 percent absolute decline in total number of workers over the next 20 years as discussed in Chapter 5. With the exception of North Africa and the Middle East, around two- thirds of the future growth in total GDP is a function of increased productivity per worker. In the case of China (as discussed), Eastern Europe, and Affluent Asia, growth of total GDP is totally a function of increased productivity per worker.

For North America, Western Europe, South America, Developing Asia, and India the growth in the number of workers is about one-third of the increase in total GDP; the rest is from increased productivity per worker.

Although there will be some people who disagree with these forecasts, it is worth remembering that these estimates are based on two things: first, the expected trend in the size of the labour force, something which can be forecast with reasonable confidence, and, second, the expected change in productivity per worker. The latter forecast is, of course, less reliable, but it does reflect the trends in education that are feasible in each country and therefore have a rational underpinning. Those with more ambitious forecasts clearly expect significant changes and benefits to come from the relationship between education and productivity per worker, or for the propensity for people to be employed to improve. This applies particularly to China, where the ambitious forecasts made by many are defiant of the reality that the labour force will decline in absolute number by 16 percent in the next two decades. (See "How Fast Can China's GDP and Household Incomes Really Grow?")

Table 6.1 (B) shows probably the more important (from a consumer market point of view) estimated size of the private consumption expenditure component of GDP—which is the best measure of the size and trend in the consumer markets.

It particularly demonstrates one important point that needs to be kept in mind at all times: That is the difference between percentage and absolute increases in growth rates. It is very tempting to become seduced by the often-quoted percentage rates for economic growth. What must be remembered, however, is that a high growth rate on a small base is worth *less* than a lower growth rate on a high base. This is clearly highlighted in Table 6.1 (B). This table shows the *absolute* increase in total PCE component of GDP (the real consumer market) by region, as well as the average annual real growth rates (CAGR). Particular attention is drawn to North America, Western Europe, and Affluent Asia, three regions that represent just 18 percent of the world's population but their spending power will collectively expand by US$8.3 trillion by 2032, even though they are growing at 2 percent or less per annum. This compares with India adding US$1.8 trillion at a 4.9 percent annual growth rate and China adding US$3.1 trillion with 4.1 percent growth

Table 6.1   Estimated and Projected Total Real GDP (A) and PCE (B) for 2012 and 2032 by Region

(A)	Total Real GDP in US$ Bns 2010 Values		CAGR 2012–2032	Absolute Increase	Share of Increase
	2012	2032			
North America	16,613	23,131	1.7%	6,518	20%
Western Europe	16,177	18,244	0.6%	2,067	6%
Affluent Asia	9,064	13,409	2.0%	4,346	14%
South America	4,981	8,535	2.7%	3,554	11%
Eastern Europe	4,011	6,029	2.1%	2,018	6%
North Africa/ Middle East	2,006	3,173	2.3%	1,168	4%
China	7,446	14,011	3.2%	6,565	21%
Developing Asia	2,112	4,321	3.6%	2,209	7%
India	1,979	5,422	5.2%	3,443	11%
Total	64,388	96,275	2.0%	31,887	100%

(B)	Total Real Private Consumption Expenditure US$ Bns		CAGR 2012–2032	Absolute Increase	Share of Increase
	2012	2032			
North America	11,562	16,174	1.7%	4,613	25%
Western Europe	9,327	10,484	0.6%	1,157	6%
Affluent Asia	5,236	7,743	2.0%	2,506	14%
South America	3,033	5,105	2.6%	2,072	11%
Eastern Europe	2,324	3,389	1.9%	1,065	6%
North Africa/ Middle East	1,049	1,663	2.3%	613	3%
China	2,499	5,558	4.1%	3,059	17%
Developing Asia	1,295	2,582	3.5%	1,287	7%
India	1,132	2,937	4.9%	1,805	10%
Total	37,457	55,634	2.0%	18,229	100%

SOURCE: Global Demographics Ltd.

rate per annum. It may be that the cash cows are a better target market and opportunity than the traditional view of emerging markets with their high growth rates but lower per customer delivery—particularly on a per household basis, as detailed in Table 6.2.

How Fast Can China's GDP and Household Incomes Really Grow?

To some extent China has become a growth cult. Based on forecasts reported by various institutions the expectation has been created that China will have no difficulty continuing to grow its total real GDP at 8 percent per annum for the next decade to 2022.

However, working with the underlying demographics and trends in education, productivity, and workforce structure, we are inclined to disagree and this note is intended to outline the reasons why economic growth might change to a slower rate.

The factors that need to be considered—and which are changing in nature—are as follows:

- The overall size of the labour force
- The skill set of the labour force
- The role of rural migrants
- Productivity per worker

Every single one of these variables is changing in direction/trend/rate, and the combined effect is considerable and not nearly as positive as others seem to believe. The phrase *perfect storm* does come to mind in this context.

Overall Size of the Labour Force

This is an input that can be measured with quite high reliability. The age profile of the population is well documented and there are sufficient cross checks to have confidence in the estimates of the number of persons who are aged 15 to 64 years (working age) and the propensity of those same people to be employed. Given that China already has one of the highest propensity to be employed rates in the world for each of males and females, there are good grounds for arguing that propensity to be employed will more likely decrease (albeit marginally) than increase.

Combining the working age population with the trends in propensity to be employed gives us the expected size of the labour force if the existing levels of employment continue (i.e., those seeking work get work at the same rate as historically) which in itself is under threat due to reduced demand for consumer products elsewhere in the world.

Based on that, the total number of employed persons changes quite dramatically over the next two decades and, as shown in Table 6.2, has a very different pattern from that of the previous decade. For the decade 2000 to 2010 (when number of employed persons peaked) the number of employed persons grew by 4.2 million per annum although the rate slowed dramatically in the last 5 years to 2.0 million extra workers per annum. For the period 2012 to 2022 it declines by an average of 4.7 million per annum, and then by an average of 8.7 million per annum for the subsequent decade. This is a given, and whatever forecasts one makes for China's GDP must factor in the declining number of workers. To gain an understanding of its significance, consider the following almost inevitable statistic. Between 2012 and 2032, China's total labour force will decline by 18.0 percent.

Table 6.2   Historic and Projected Trend in the Size of China's Labour Force

		2002	2007	2012	2017	2022	2027	2032
Persons of working age	Mns	910.0	957.2	987.7	975.7	947.9	910.4	850.4
Propensity to be employed		81%	79%	77%	76%	75%	75%	74%
Employed persons	Mns	737.4	753.2	760.9	746.2	713.6	678.6	626.3
Urban employed	Mns	309.7	368.3	433.3	473.7	495.8	502.2	493.9

SOURCE: Global Demographics Ltd.

The Skill Set of the Labour Force

This is important, as it impacts productivity. Within individual countries, there is a good relationship over time between overall education standard of the workforce and productivity of the

(*Continued*)

workforce, and while there are significant differences between countries in terms of the extent to which they are able to leverage that relationship, China has been amongst the best.

In the case of China, the increase in standard of education over the last two decades has been very good, with the index value in the last seven years rising from 158 to 178—and this is expected to continue for the simple reason that the education facilities are in place and the demand on them is reducing. But the impact of the new entrants to the adult population and, hence, labour force on the overall education standard of the labour force is reducing. While the new entrants are increasingly better educated than those presently in the workforce, there are fewer new entrants each year. The number of new entrants to adults in 2002 was 22 million—by 2012 this has dropped to 16 million and by 2032 it is 12 million.

As such, the incremental gain in overall skill levels is slowing and this impacts the rate at which gains are achieved in productivity per worker. The pattern of the national education index and its relationship with productivity per worker (GDP divided by number of employed persons) is shown in Figure 6.5.

Basically, the historical relationship indicates one of three scenarios. Linear is the line that grows the least by 2022 and is actually the best statistical fit for 2005 to 2012. Second, there is a power function—which rises steadily though to 2022. Then there is the middle case. The middle case is the expected outcome, as it is the sum of the individual provinces and reflects that some provinces have reached the point where faster growth will be achieved (i.e., passed the 200 mark on the education index and therefore justify the use of a power function for the forecast), and others which are still a long way below that level and for which productivity growth will be slow (linear function for forecast).

This means that the output per worker will increase but the rate of increase will in all probability be slower than what it has

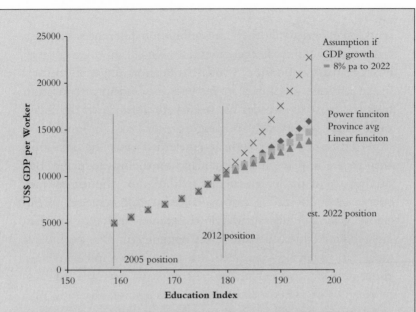

Figure 6.5 The Historical and Forecast Relationship between Education Standard of Adults and Productivity per Worker

been in the past. For it to be faster is to assume some new intervening factor.

That brings us to the steeply rising line in Figure 6.5. This is the required trend in GDP per worker relative to education if the total real GDP is to grow at an average of 8 percent per annum for the next decade to 2022 (when the education index for all China will have reached 195). It clearly assumes some major change in the relationship between skill, capital per worker, and productivity per worker. Just what this change might be is unclear and perhaps for that reason that forecast should be treated with care.

The Rural Migrant

One option that is frequently mentioned as such an intervening factor is the rural to urban migrant. One suspects that it is resorted to because estimates of the size of this group have been anecdotal and many brave assumptions can be made without

(Continued)

evidence to support them. It is useful, therefore, to examine the nature of rural to urban migration.

There are, of course, good grounds for claiming that persons that move from rural to urban work are more productive, and that is not in dispute. What is in dispute is the continuation of this movement and its absolute significance.

There are two versions of rural to urban migration—the short-term, less, than six months migrant, and the permanent migrant. There are actually good data on the number of permanent migrants, as people must register with the Public Security Bureau if they move into a county different from their birth county for more than six months. The data on this are publically available, and from that it is possible to derive the exact profile of the nature of persons who have moved from rural to urban areas for more than six months. In that respect the following points should be noted. Historically (and probably a function of the improving quality of education in even the rural areas), a rural-born person who turns 15 has a 50 percent likelihood of being permanently in an urban area within 10 years, and by the time he or she reaches age 30 it is 73 percent. This does mean that over the last 20 years the rural areas have been effectively hollowed out in terms of the young (family stage) adults. In 2010, the difference between the age profile of urban and rural populations of China is significant— and the majority of births are now urban rather than rural. This, in turn, means the key supply factor for rural urban long-term migrants—that is, the number of people turning 15—has been and will continue to be in steady decline from 17 million in 2002 to 9 million in 2012 and a projected 4 million by 2032. This is a good indicator of the number of persons that will migrate each year and their absolute number. In that respect there are two clear findings. First, the number will decline— effectively halving over the next two decades. The only possible exception to that is if the older rural resident (40+ years) suddenly decides to move to urban areas—but given their failure to do so at this time and their lower skill level (they are less well educated), this is unlikely to happen.

Second, it should be observed that the number migrating is not significant in the context of the total labour force to materially alter average productivity of the total labour force. In 2012, the total employed labour force is 761 million persons, and 43 percent of them are rural workers. This means there is an estimated 433 million urban workers in place and the long-term rural urban migrants in that year are estimated at 12 million. (Note this is higher than the number of rural persons turning 15 years of age referred to previously, as it includes persons of all ages who migrated in 2012.) That makes them 2 percent of the urban labour force if all the migrants work (the majority will). Is it credible to claim that 3 percent of the youngest, least-experienced and least well-educated entrants to the urban labour force will result in a significant (or even measurable) increase in productivity per worker? We think not.

The other aspect of rural urban migration is the temporary migrant (fewer than six months). These are farm workers moving to urban areas in the winter when there is less demand for their labour in rural areas and they typically are engaged in labouring jobs in urban areas. While serving a useful role, the reality is that their productivity is not increased a lot—it is still manual labour. Furthermore, they do not contribute to the urban economy—they live minimally and save as much as they can for looking after their family in the rural village. So again, the expectation that these older rural workers will significantly lift productivity is perhaps ambitious if not wishful in nature.

Productivity per Worker

This then is the critical variable. Consider the plot so far. Total workers are now in decline. Urban-based workers (the more productive) are still increasing—but whereas they grew by 12 million per annum for the last decade (approximately 3.4 percent

(Continued)

per annum), they can now be expected to grow at a more sedate 6.2 million per annum over the next decade—which is 1.3 percent per annum. A drop of 2 percentage points. At the same time, the overall educational quality of the labour force is not growing at the same rate. In the decade to 2012, the education index increased by 1.65 percent per annum. For the next two decades, it will now grow at a much slower 0.9 percent per annum.

So what does this mean for overall productivity of the labour force? For the last decade the education index grew at 1.65 percent per annum and the productivity per worker grew at 9.9 percent per annum. For the next decade the education index is projected to improve at 0.9 percent per annum, and as a result productivity will grow at a slower rate than before—with our most likely estimate being 4.8 percent. The subsequent decade is projected to be almost the same in terms of rate of change.

Which leads to the final figure—total real GDP. This is productivity per worker (increasing at 4.5 percent per annum) multiplied by number of workers (decreasing at 0.9 percent per annum), which gives a total real GDP growth rate for the next 20 years of 3.4 percent per annum. This, of course, is very different from other forecasts, but there is a rationale behind it.

The Future for Household Incomes

Having assessed by country or region how much total GDP and PCE will grow, the next question to consider is, what does this mean for household incomes? Table 6.3 compares average household income by region in 2012 and 2032 as estimated from the PCE divided by number of households and adjusted for propensity to spend and tax rates by income level by country. Not surprisingly, average household incomes are expected to increase in real terms by 2032 everywhere. The average

Table 6.3 Estimated and Projected Average Household Income in 2012 and 2032 (US$ pa)

| | Average Real Household Incomes US$ pa 2010 Values | | CAGR | Absolute |
	2012	2032	2012–2032	Increase
North America	116,128	136,162	0.8%	20,034
Western Europe	77,138	79,781	0.2%	2,643
Affluent Asia	89,403	123,372	1.6%	33,969
South America	28,240	40,170	1.8%	11,930
Eastern Europe	22,670	33,433	2.0%	10,763
North Africa/Middle East	16,716	16,963	0.1%	247
China	9,674	29,143	5.7%	19469
Developing Asia	8,276	12,528	2.1%	4,252
India	5,724	11,892	3.7%	6,168
Total	32,157	43,494	1.4%	10,282

SOURCE: Global Demographics Ltd.

is expected to increase from US$32,157 per annum in 2012 to reach US$43,494 in 2032 (in real 2010 values). This is an annual growth rate of 1.52 percent. Clearly, China has the highest growth rate: at 5.7 percent per annum for the next 20 years. This reflects a combination of an increasing productivity per worker and an increasing private consumption share of the total GDP, as a result of real wage inflation due to an increasing shortage of workers and higher minimum wage levels. It is important to note the change in the share of China's GDP accounted for by private consumption. Currently, this is 33 percent; however, the stated objective of the Chinese government is to raise this percentage. As a result, our model assumes it will reach 40 percent by 2032 meaning that consumption will grow faster than the overall economy, with obvious implications for the growth in household incomes as shown in Table 6.3.

In real terms, China's (real 2010 values) average household incomes will more than double by 2032, from US$9,674 to US$29,143. India has the second highest growth rate at 3.72 percent per annum, which is a function of the increasing number of employed persons per household and increasing education with its consequent impact on productivity per worker. As a result, the average real household income in India also is projected to double in the next 20 years from US$5,724 to US$11,892 in 2032.

Once again, it is useful to look beyond growth rates and consider absolute changes. China has by far the highest annual average growth rate in household incomes but, in terms of the absolute increase in average per household income, Affluent Asia is highest at US$33,969 followed by North America at US$20,034 between 2012 and 2032. China's increase of US$19,469 and India's of US$6,168 is smaller.

However, these different growth rates do impact on the share of total earned incomes that each region accounts for and, thereby, its absolute importance as a consumer market. This is shown in Figure 6.6. The reader is reminded that total earned income is the average household income for each country multiplied by the number of households

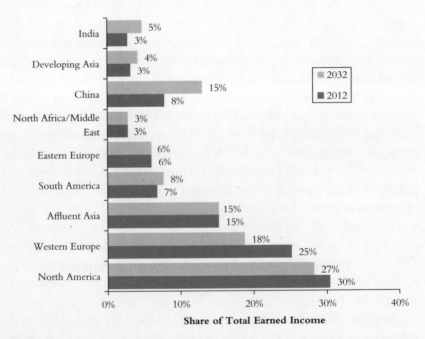

Figure 6.6 Share of Total Earned Household Incomes by Region, 2012 and 2032

Source: Global Demographics Ltd.

in the country—summed for all countries in the region. It is a reliable measure of the real spending power of a country or region.

While there are some interesting changes that are expected to take place, perhaps the most important point is that while the projected percentages may alter, the relative positions of each of the regions do not. Clearly, the increased importance of India and China is significant. Collectively, they will increase from 11 percent of the global consumer incomes (and by implication, spending power) to reach 20 percent. In contrast the three affluent regions (and particularly North America and Western Europe) will decline from 71 percent of the total to 60 percent.

However, it is important that the reader notes that these affluent regions nonetheless grow in absolute value of earned incomes—just at a slower pace. The fascination with growth rates means that real absolute growth gets overlooked—and yet that is the real market opportunity. As shown in the bottom half of Table 6.1, while the affluent parts of the world, with 18 percent of the population, have growth in total expenditure of less than 2 percent per annum, they nonetheless are projected to account for 45 percent of the global increase in consumer spending over the next decade. This compares with China at 17 percent share of increased consumer expenditure (with 23 percent of global population) and 10 percent for India (with 21 percent of the global population). Clearly, these differences in share of spending and share of population have significant implications for profit margin per customer.

Basically, nearly half the extra spending power in the world over the next two decades will be in North America, Affluent Asia, and Western Europe—and this is where the older empty nester consumer segment is dominant and, given the higher revenue per customer, will be where the profit is.

Deciding Whether to Save or Spend

Finally, in this chapter looking at household incomes, it is useful to understand the relationship between income and spending, across countries and regions. This is discussed in greater detail in Chapter 8 but there is value in understanding it here as it helps relate incomes to market size.

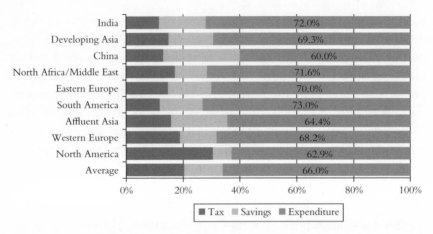

Figure 6.7   Propensity to Spend, 2012
Source: Global Demographics Ltd.

Figure 6.7 shows for each region/country the proportion of gross household income that is actually spent, given prevailing tax rates and the propensity to save. As shown, average tax rates on household income vary significantly, from a low of 12 percent in India to a high of 30 percent in North America. Due to the popularity of progressive taxation, higher tax rates in North America and Western Europe are a reflection of their higher average incomes. Where tax is concerned, consumers have very little discretion over whether to pay them; in other words, this is an element of nondiscretionary expenditure which is going to happen. This contrasts with the savings rate, which is more of a discretionary choice made by each wage earner. However, it is important to recognise that the means of saving differ widely between economies. For example, in the developed world, a well-established mortgage industry encourages households to borrow a mortgage to buy an expensive asset (a house), paying a part off each year. This payment is recorded as expenditure. However, in poorer countries, the household must save up for the house before buying it—and this is recorded as savings. In both cases, households are putting money aside for a capital asset, yet analysts record one as expenditure and the other as savings, then chastise Western economies for being poor savers.

Adjusting for anomalies in tax and savings rates reveals a degree of similarity across regions in terms of the proportion of income that is available for spending. Typically, a household gets to spend 66 percent of its gross income irrespective of the average income in the country/region it is located. This, perhaps, is not surprising as there is a degree of offset between tax and need to save. Western Europe is a good example—higher taxes but much higher availability of free social services, such as health and education—so the need to save is reduced. This compares with China, where health care is still very much a user-pays scenario, and with an ageing population the need to provide for that encourages a higher savings rate.

So, referring to the second half of Table 6.1, which shows the absolute amount of household expenditure in each region, it explains to some extent the greater importance of the affluent economies. It also helps explains why China's total level of consumer spending will grow rapidly. Part of it will be a shift of the economy to the consumer, thereby lifting incomes and spending, and part will be a shift from saving to mortgages. As a consequence, a significant change for China will be that the world will come to view China less as a place to buy things from and more as a place to sell things to.

Summary

The potential opportunities created by different markets are very much a function of the amount of money they earn, the proportion of that which is available to spend after tax, and the need to save. The opportunity varies substantially by region, reflecting differences in earning power (productivity) and number of households. While Western Europe, North America, and Affluent Asia may account for only 18 percent of the population of all regions included in this study, because of their much higher productivity they account for 71 percent of the total earned income and 70 percent of total consumer expenditure in the world. For any company to have a successful global presence, it must have a strong position in these markets.

It is clear that India and China have much faster growth rates in terms of total earned incomes and total consumer expenditure over the next two decades. However, this chapter demonstrates strongly why one should not be persuaded by the mantra of growth rates. They represent just 8 percent and 3 percent of global consumer income today (2012), and even with projected growth rates of consumer income of over 4 percent per annum for the next two decades (compared with less than 2 percent per annum for the three affluent regions), they nonetheless achieve only 15 percent and 5 percent of total global consumer incomes in 2032—and account for only 27 percent of growth in total global consumer spending. So, yes, important markets and growing—but they are not an answer in themselves. A company needs to consider its cash cows and protect its position there before focusing on these smaller growth markets.

The next chapter focuses on the distribution of income in society and, in particular, what it means to be part of the fast-growing and increasingly significant middle class.

Chapter 7

Distribution of Households by Income

In the previous chapter we looked at the aggregate amount of household income, explaining where it is located and how the current picture can be expected to change in the future. This provides us with a picture of the total earning power of each region, as well as of individual economies. This chapter looks at the distribution of households by income within a region/country. We will do this in two ways. First, we will consider earned income, because that is currently how most people define their markets. Second, we will look at the distribution of spending, as societies have different incomes, tax rates, and cultural attitudes to saving. This latter approach is a more meaningful way to assess the potential for a market.

Introduction

The global distribution of households by income is best shown using a semi-logarithmic scale. This means that the step size at the lower end of the scale is smaller than the step size at the upper end—with a steady progression in the increase of step size from the bottom to the top. That then means we have adequate detail for poor countries where the range of incomes is small—typically between zero and US$10,000, and similarly the larger steps at the top end provide detail on the distribution of households by income in the affluent countries where the range is from US$25,000 to US$125,000. Figure 7.1 shows the global household income distribution and how it is likely to change over the next two decades. These figures do not include inflation, so the chart is showing the real changes in the distribution of households by income that is expected to take place as GDP grows.

This chart highlights the axis point between rich and poor at an annual household income of US$10,000. In other words, in the years to 2032, all the segments below that segment will decrease in size so that there are (happily) fewer poor households. Conversely, all income segments above that point are projected to increase in terms of number of households. While US$10,000 might seem a low threshold, the reality is that in 2012 an estimated 50 percent of all households in the world earn less than this amount. Furthermore, because lower income households tend to have more children in them, the proportion of the global population in this income range is 57 percent. A further 21 percent of all households earn between US$10,000 and US$25,000, making a total of 71 percent of households earning less than US$25,000.

Nearly three out of every four households in the world live on $25,000 per annum or less. This 71 percent of households account for 17 percent of the world's income or, to put it the other way round, 29 percent of households earn 83 percent of the world's income.

A different picture emerges when calculating the total earned income of the different income groups (that is, the sum of incomes of all households in each segment). The 50 percent of all households (57 percent of population) with an income below US$10,000 in 2012 account for just 11 percent of the total earned income in the world covered by this book. There is significant earning disparity throughout the world.

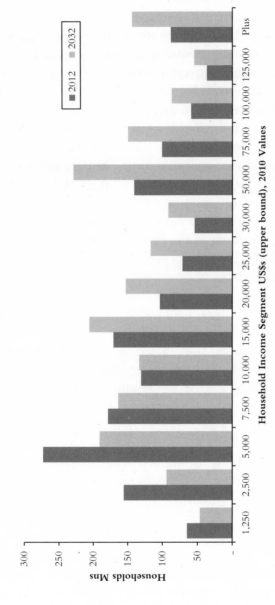

Figure 7.1 Global Distribution of Households by Income (Real 2010 US$ Values)
Source: Global Demographics Ltd.

Of course, from a sociological point of view it would be good if this disparity could be reduced and, as a result of better education leading to improved earning power in the developing world, there is an important shift taking place, which is shown in Figure 7.1. In fact, all income segments below US$7,500 to US$10,000 are projected to reduce both as a proportion of all households and in absolute number by 2032. The number of households earning up to US$10,000 will fall from 50 percent of the total number of households to 34 percent by 2032 (and from 58 percent to 43 percent of all people). Not only is this a significant reduction in terms of the share of households, it is also a 22 percent reduction in terms of the absolute number of households.

As Figure 7.1 also highlights, all income groups from US$10,000 and above are projected to increase in size over the next 20 years. The number of households earning over US$10,000 and less than US$25,000 increases from 346 million to 475 million. The US$25,000 to US$100,000 segment is projected to increase from 354 million households in 2012 to 556 million households by 2032, which as a proportion of all households takes this segment from 21 percent to 30 percent of all households. This segment is clearly going to be an important growth area during that period.

The highest income segment, those households with an income in excess of US$100,000, is projected to grow fastest from 124 million in 2012 (7.5 percent of all households) to 198 million in 2032. The economic importance of this segment is considerable. That is, the top 7.6 percent of households in 2012 currently accounts for 48 percent of all earned income, or very nearly one out of every two dollars earned. By 2032 this is expected to increase to 10 percent of all households accounting for 52 percent of earned income. While this may be a small segment in terms of the total number of households, it will be very important to global consumption and savings, being just under half of all earned income in the countries covered.

The Different Income Segments

So what are the income segments? In order to keep the analysis comprehensible, four income segments are used as follows:

1. The lowest, which is households with an annual income below US$15,000. It is 60 percent of households in 2012 but drops to 45 percent by 2032.

2. Households with an annual income between US$15,000 and US$50,000. This is 23 percent of all households in 2012 increasing to 32 percent by 2032. That is growing from 369 million to 590 million households in 20 years, a 60 percent increase in segment size.

3. Households with an annual household income between US$50,000 and US$100,000. In 2012 this is estimated to include 10 percent of all households, increasing to 13 percent by 2032. In absolute number it contains 160 million households now, increasing to 236 million by 2032, a 48 percent increase.

4. The affluent, with an annual household income over US$100,000. This is the top 8 percent of households in 2012 and increases to 10.7 percent by 2032, taking it from 124 million to 198 million affluent households, a 60 percent increase in absolute size.

Analysis of the Income Segments

There are three ways in which these segments should be examined. The first is in terms of the share of each income segment that is accounted for by each region. Basically, this helps determine which regions a particular product or service should focus on given its potential price point and target market. The second is to look at the share of each region that each income segment accounts for. This helps identify the share of households within a region/country that a particular product or service can reach at a specific price point.

The third is to look at the value of each segment. That is the total earned income of all households in the segment. This is important because the previous two look at households; this looks at revenue and hence profit potential. Compare, for example, the top income segment with the US$15,000 to US$50,000 income segment. The relative size in terms of households and share of earned income of each segment for each of 2012 and 2032 and implications in terms of change is shown in Table 7.1. The highest income segment is only 8 percent of households but accounts for a very significant 48 percent of the earned income in the world. These proportions change to 11 percent and 52 percent, respectively, by 2032. More important, while it is only 8 percent of households in 2012, it will account for 59 percent of the increase in spending power over the next two decades. This contrasts with the US$15,000 to US$50,000 segment, which has a very significant increase in number of households (adding

Table 7.1 Relative Size of Income Segments in Terms of Share of Households and Share of Earned Income, 2012 and 2032

	Income Segments			
	US$0–15,000	US$15,000–50,000	US$50,000–100,000	US$100,000 +
Share of Households				
2012	59.8%	22.7%	9.8%	7.6%
2032	44.9%	31.7%	12.7%	10.7%
Households (Millions)				
2012	974	370	159	124
2032	834	590	236	198
Change Households (Millions)	−140	220	77	74
Share of Earned Income				
2012	11%	20%	21%	48%
2032	7%	21%	21%	52%
Earned Income US$ (Billions)				
2012	5,610	10,309	11,241	25,158
2032	5,589	16,602	16,604	42,081
Change US$ (Billions)	−20	6,293	5,363	16,923

SOURCE: Global Demographics Ltd.

220 million on a current base of 370 million) but which accounts for just 22 percent of the increase in earned income in the world.

These two segments demonstrate quite strongly the vanity versus sanity debate. Much has been made of entering markets with huge growth in numbers of consumers such as the US$15,000 to US$50,000 segment, which will have a further 220 million households by 2032, but there has been less discussion than perhaps warranted on the profit potential of these customers and hence markets. Those who focus on the market levels at which they can make a profit are perhaps the better bet than those who claim massive numbers of customers but little profit per customer. The top income segment might only add 74 million households but will account for a massive 59 percent of the increase in total earned incomes in the world.

Regional Share of Income Segments

There are significant differences in terms of regional presence in each segment and how this will change over the next two decades, which is examined in Figures 7.2 to 7.5, starting with the lowest income segment in 2012 being those households with an income below US$15,000. As shown in Figure 7.2 (A) 79 percent are located in India, China, and Developing Asia. A further 6 percent are in Africa and the Middle East with another 8 percent in Eastern Europe. Over half these households are living on less than US$2.50 per day per capita.

Figure 7.2 (B) shows the situation in 2032. The change in the regional distribution of the lower-income households is dramatic, mainly as a result of the favorable projections for China's economic growth and the proportion of its households moving up to higher income segments relative to other countries and regions. By 2032, China's share of the number of households earning less than US$15,000 per annum is projected to fall from today's 37 percent to just 23 percent. In fact, China accounts for most (92 percent) of the projected decrease in the absolute number of households in this segment. This contrasts with the situation in India,

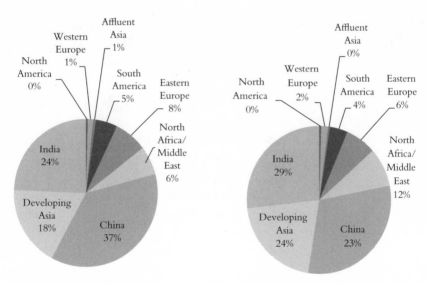

Figure 7.2 2012 (A) and 2032 (B) Regional Distribution of Households with Incomes Below $15,000
Source: Global Demographics Ltd.

which is forecast to achieve very little improvement, with over 242 million households remaining in this segment in the years to 2032. Unfortunately, the news in this aspect is not looking good either in North Africa and the Middle East, with their presence in this segment rising from 6 percent of the global total to 12 percent by 2032.

The next group of households that is changing fast is the segment earning US$15,000 to US$50,000. These are often referred to as the *emerging middle class*. This is projected to increase from 23 percent of all households to 32 percent by 2032, with the addition of 220 million households, an increase of 60 percent in absolute segment size. This segment accounts for an estimated 20 percent of total earned incomes in the world in 2012, and that proportion is projected to increase to 21 percent over the next 20 years.

As shown in Figure 7.3 (A), China accounts for nearly one fifth of all households in this segment in 2012 and is projected to increase to nearly one third of the segment over the next 20 years reflecting a significant shift in number of households from the lower income segment up to this segment. Another difference in this segment from the previous is the increased presence of regions outside Asia, notably South America and Eastern Europe. Taken together in 2012, they are 31 percent of this segment, whereas they only accounted for 13 percent of the lower-income segment.

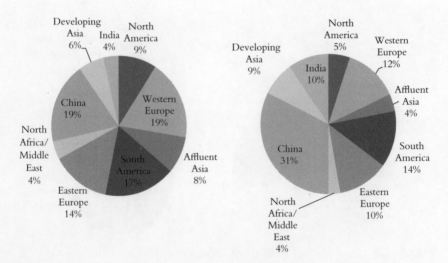

Figure 7.3   2012 (A) and 2032 (B) Regional Distribution of Households with Incomes between US$15,000 and US$50,000 in Real 2010 US$ Values
Source: Global Demographics Ltd.

Over the next 20 years it is expected that India will increase its share of this segment together with Developing Asia, as shown in Figure 7.3 (B). India will move from having 13.5 million households in the US$15,000 to US$50,000 segment (4 percent of the global total) to 63 million (10 percent); Developing Asia will rise from 23 million (6 percent) to 53 million (9 percent); while in North Africa and the Middle East the change will be from 16 million (4 percent) to 23 million (4 percent). As mentioned previously, this progress is largely due to economic growth in these regions, and over the next two decades many households will move up to earn more than US$15,000.

The next segment to consider is those households with annual earnings between US$50,000 and US$100,000, which is the true middle class by international standards. That is, close to one third of USA households are earning below or above this range. The number of households in this segment is expected to increase by 48 percent from 159 million in 2012 to 236 million by 2032. As a proportion of all households, this segment is likely to increase from 10 percent in 2012 to 13 percent by 2032, which is not a significant change. However, while its share of all households is quite stable, its composition by region is changing dramatically, as highlighted in Figure 7.4 (A & B).

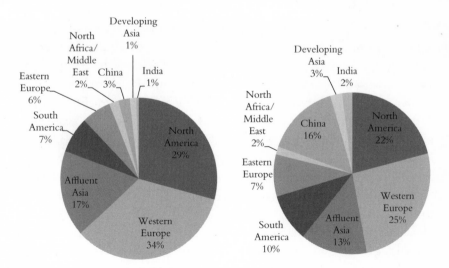

Figure 7.4 2012 (A) and 2032 (B) Regional Distribution of Households with Incomes between US$50,000 and US$100,000 in Real 2010 US$ Values
Source: Global Demographics Ltd.

Several points are particularly significant. First, the mix of countries in 2012 is very different from the previous two income segments. North America, Western Europe, and Affluent Asia dominate this segment accounting for 80 percent of such households in 2012. But, by 2032, even though the number of households in these regions in this income range increases marginally, this has reduced to 59 percent as a result of growth of presence of the other regions in this income segment.

China, which is just 3 percent of this segment in 2012, is projected to be 16 percent by 2032, making it a significant player in this income segment. Eastern Europe and South America in aggregate increase from 13 percent to 17 percent of this segment. So clearly this income segment develops a very different geographical focus.

In the next 20 years, it is expected that China will increase from 3 percent to 13 percent of all households with an annual income between US$50,000 and US$100,000, while the three affluent regions (Western Europe, Affluent Asia, and North America) will reduce in proportion from 81 percent to 61 percent

Finally, we come to the highest income segment: those households earning more than US$100,000 per annum. These are estimated to be 8 percent (124 million) of all households in 2012 and projected to increase to 11 percent (198 million) by 2032 under the GDP growth scenarios detailed in the previous chapter. This is a 60 percent increase in absolute numbers. Figure 7.5 (A & B) shows the composition of this income segment in terms of regional presence, and the dominance of North America, Western Europe, and Affluent Asia. In 2012 they are 91 percent of all such households and even by 2032 they dominate at 79 percent. China is expected to increase from less than 1 percent of this income segment to 9 percent. Translated into actual numbers, this means that China is expected to go from having 959,000 households earning more than US$100,000 before tax each year to 17.7 million by 2032—an additional 17 million such households. However, do note that over the same time period the number of households with an income in excess of US$100,000 increases by 23 million in North America, 15 million in Affluent Asia, and 5 million in Western Europe. In short, 58 percent of the increase in affluent

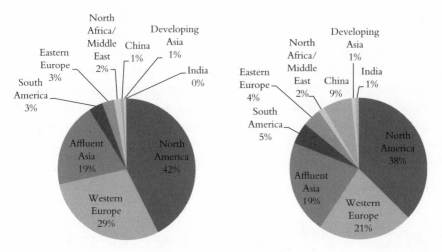

Figure 7.5   2012 (A) and 2032 (B) Regional Distribution of Households with Incomes over US$100,000 in Real 2010 US$ Values
Source: Global Demographics Ltd.

households takes place in those three regions. Most other regions gain only about 1 percent point share of the affluent over the next 20 years.

Clearly, if a firm wants to reach those households earning more than US$100,000 per year, then it needs to focus first on the developed world. Only once it has optimised operations there should it develop a strategy for engaging the affluent in China. Most of the rest of the world is much less significant for this segment. Fortunately, most of China's households in this segment are concentrated in a relatively small number of cities, so that distribution focused on a few locations can reach a high proportion of these very affluent Chinese (see Chapter 10). The same applies to India in this respect, which is expected to have 1.6 million households in this income segment by 2032.

As well as looking at the obvious issue of where different income segments are located, it is also worth pausing to consider the differences in demographic profile of each income segment. The lowest income segment (under US$15,000), which is currently dominated by China, India, and Developing Asia, is perhaps slightly dichotomous in nature. In China, for reasons discussed, households consist of two adults and typically one child, with just under half the households having no child at all. For India (and Developing Asia) the opposite profile exists and families have two or three children, so they are younger and have a particularly low per capita income (as the household size is larger). The picture is markedly different at the other end of the spectrum among those households with incomes in excess of $100,000. Their household size is usually small and more likely to be childless, so their level of discretionary spending is significantly greater. Individuals in this segment tend to be older, typically over 40.

Income Segment Share of Each Region

It is also revealing to understand how the proportion of households in each of the four income segments varies across regions, and how this is likely to alter over the next two decades. This information helps to reveal where broad commercial opportunities lie and how the character of each region will develop. This situation is highlighted in Figure 7.6 (A & B).

The dichotomy between regions is clearly evident. In 2012, India, Developing Asia, China, and the Middle East have particularly high proportions of poor households. This contrasts with North America, Western Europe, and Affluent Asia, which have at least a fifth of their households in the US$100,000 plus segment and over 50 percent in the US$50,000 plus segments. South America, just as it does for age, sits between these two groups. Clearly, the lifestyles of the average consumer in each of these different worlds varies enormously, as does the potential profit per customer compared with the more frequently touted, but less important, number of customers.

Because percentages do not always show the absolute dynamics of a market, Table 7.2 shows the absolute change in number of households by income segment by region. This, if nothing else, explains the fascination with the change that is happening in China and, to a lesser extent, Developing Asia and India. In the next two decades, under the GDP growth assumptions explained in the previous chapter, the number of households in China with an income in excess of US$15,000 in 2010 values will increase by 162 million over a current base of 74 million. For India it is 55 million over a base of 14.5 million, and for Developing Asia it is 36 million over a base of 25 million in 2012.

The Relative Value of the Income Segments

The previous two sections of this chapter looked at the absolute and relative size of the different income segments in terms of number of

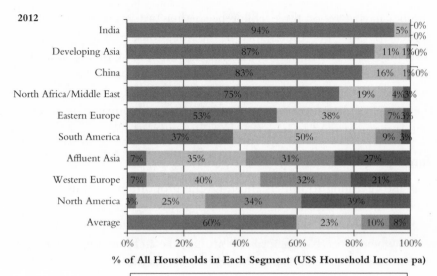

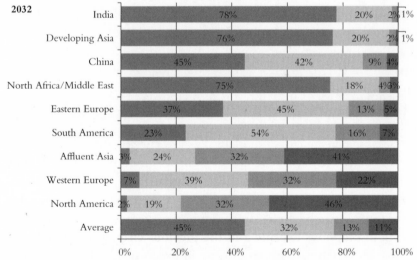

Figure 7.6   2012 (A) and 2032 (B) Proportion of Each Region within Each Income Segment
Source: Global Demographics Ltd.

Table 7.2   Number of Households (Millions) Entering or Leaving Each Income Segment over the Next 20 Years (2012–2032)

	Number of Households (Millions) Entering/Leaving Segment between 2012 and 2032			
	Income Segments			
	US$0–15,000	US$15,000–50,000	US$50,000–100,000	US$100,000 +
North America	−522	−1,931	5,558	22,988
Western Europe	851	3,932	4,185	5,215
Affluent Asia	−2,983	−9,001	2,661	14,836
South America	−11,971	17,731	12,336	5,928
Eastern Europe	−22,387	9,902	7,790	3,833
North Africa/ Middle East	35,171	7,056	2,032	1,609
China	−167,321	112,869	32,931	16,734
Developing Asia	24,625	30,435	4,304	1,437
India	4,581	49,093	4,785	1,425
Total	−139,955	220,086	76,580	74,005

SOURCE: Global Demographics Ltd.

households in them first in terms of regions presence in each segment and then second, each segment's presence in each region (i.e., what proportion of North American households earn over US$100,000). This analysis is useful in terms of measuring the number of potential customers. However, it is also very important to understand the value of the different income segments. That is, the sum of the incomes of households in each segment. This is more important as it shows the potential revenue that can be earned from each and where the real value growth (sanity) is rather than customer volume growth (vanity).

Over the next 20 years, the total earned income of all households in the countries/regions covered is projected to increase from US$52,318 billion in 2012 to US$80,876 billion.

Over the next 20 years, the total earned income of all households in the countries/regions covered, is projected to increase from US$52,318 billion in 2012 to US$80,876 billion. This is a significant increase, 55 percent in absolute terms. The first part of Table 7.3 shows the total value of each segment by region in 2012 and the second part shows the percent of total increase of this by 2032 that is accounted for by each region/segment.

This shows that in 2012 an estimated 48 percent of the total earned income of households in the regions covered is earned by households with an annual income in excess of US$100,000. That is, US$25,158 billion out of a total earned income of all households in 2012 of US$52,318 billion. Furthermore, most of those households (as shown earlier in this chapter) are located in North America, Western Europe, and Affluent Asia. Also, it is significant from a business strategy point of view to note that these same segments account for 38 percent of the total increase in earned incomes of all the regions covered. So, two fifths of the growth in the world's consumption power is located in affluent households in those three regions. The US$100,000 plus household in China accounts for a further 13 percent of global growth in earned income and then South America at 4 percent and Eastern Europe at 2 percent.

The other high-growth income segment in terms of share of increase in total earned income over the next 20 years is the US$15,000 to US$50,000—which accounts for 22 percent of the projected increase in total earned incomes. This is clearly dominated by China, then India, Developing Asia, and South America.

The choice of where to target of course depends on the nature of the company and product or service being offered. However, the important point to be made here is that, as shown in the third part of Table 7.3, while there is significant growth in the number of households in the lower tier income segment (US$15,000 to US$50,000) the revenue per customer is much lower, as is growth in absolute value terms (22 percent of total market growth compared with 59 percent for the highest income segment).

Who Are the Middle Class?

Understanding the global distribution of incomes is useful, but it is important to remember that there are significant differences between countries in their patterns of consumption, tax rates, and propensity to

Table 7.3 The Value of Each Income Segment/Region, Share of Change Accounted for by Each and Average Income per Household in Each Segment

	Income Segments				
	US$0– 15,000	US$15,000– 50,000	US$50,000– 100,000	US$100,000 +	Total
Total Earned Income (US$Bn) of Each Segment/Region 2012					
North America	42	1,149	3,370	11,312	15,873
Western Europe	114	2,233	3,812	6,986	13,145
Affluent Asia	58	998	1,945	4,952	7,953
South America	428	1,693	778	647	3,546
Eastern Europe	555	1,388	640	559	3,142
North Africa/ Middle East	290	404	216	461	1,371
China	2,195	1,595	283	127	4,200
Developing Asia	869	544	144	90	1,646
India	1,060	305	53	24	1,442
Total	5,610	10,309	11,241	25,158	52,318
Share of Change in Total Earned Income by Region 2012–2032					
North America	0.0%	−0.2%	1.6%	20.7%	22.0%
Western Europe	0.0%	0.4%	1.1%	4.0%	5.5%
Affluent Asia	−0.1%	−0.9%	0.8%	13.2%	13.0%
South America	−0.3%	2.2%	3.0%	3.8%	8.6%
Eastern Europe	−0.5%	1.3%	1.9%	2.5%	5.1%
North Africa/ Middle East	0.5%	0.6%	0.5%	1.2%	2.8%
China	−2.7%	11.6%	7.9%	12.6%	29.4%
Developing Asia	1.1%	2.7%	1.0%	0.8%	5.6%
India	2.0%	4.2%	1.1%	0.6%	7.9%
Total	−0.1%	22.0%	18.8%	59.3%	100.0%
Income per Household by Income Segment in 2012					
North America	10,037	34,202	72,779	214,963	116,128
Western Europe	9,811	32,553	70,422	193,717	77,138
Affluent Asia	9,681	31,774	70,415	206,788	89,403
South America	9,106	26,894	67,464	159,354	28,240
Eastern Europe	7,568	26,513	67,466	160,720	22,671
North Africa/ Middle East	4,731	26,009	68,675	221,023	16,716
China	6,106	23,114	65,756	132,284	9,682
Developing Asia	5,006	24,024	66,533	137,815	8,276
India	4,466	22,486	65,700	117,997	5,724
Total	5,762	27,889	70,478	202,765	32,159

save. These complications matter because they make it a little harder to compare the attractiveness of different markets. It also creates confusion when people use the term *middle class*, a significant number of people widely thought to have significant amounts of discretionary spending.

To throw some light on this matter we will put some actual numbers to this term. To begin we will first use what seems to be the most widely accepted approach, which is to define middle class as households with an income level ranging from a minimum of US$10 income per day per capita to a maximum of US$100 per day per capita (above that the household is classified as affluent). Adjustment needs to be made in this case for purchasing power parity (PPP) as the objective here is to try and compare lifestyle rather than market size. (See comment on purchasing power parity and market sizing later in this chapter.)

Figure 7.7 shows graphically the proportion of households that fall within this definition by region in 2012 after adjusting for purchasing power parity and household size. Some claim that this indicates a very significant middle class in India and China. However, this approach does have a potential flaw. The lower limit of US$10 per person per day spending power (income) means that a household in Western Europe with an average household size of 2.4 persons meets these criteria with a total annual household income of US$10,700, which is 96 percent of all households in Western Europe, North America, and Affluent Asia. In Western Europe, with its highly developed social support system, it is almost impossible for a household to have an income that low. Basically a household income of US$10,700 in Europe or North America, even after adjusting for PPP (which in this case is close to 1 anyhow), is not middle class by any sensible definition.

The often-used lower limit of US$10 per person per day spending power (income) to define the start of "middle class" means that, after taking into account purchasing power parity and household size by income level, it is equivalent to a total annual household income of US$10,700 in Western Europe. In short, 96 percent of households in Western Europe are defined as middle class, which is nonsensical.

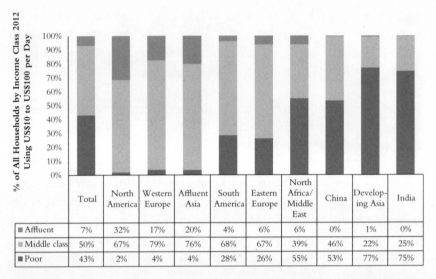

	Total	North America	Western Europe	Affluent Asia	South America	Eastern Europe	North Africa/ Middle East	China	Developing Asia	India
■ Affluent	7%	32%	17%	20%	4%	6%	6%	0%	1%	0%
■ Middle class	50%	67%	79%	76%	68%	67%	39%	46%	22%	25%
■ Poor	43%	2%	4%	4%	28%	26%	55%	53%	77%	75%

Figure 7.7   The Projected Proportion of All Households That Are Middle Class under the US$10 to US$100 Spend per Person per Day (PPP Definition)
Source: Global Demographics Ltd.

So the proposition that there is a booming middle class in Developing Asia, China, and India on the basis of these criteria is clearly wrong. Middle class has to be households with an income per capita equal to a middle class household in the developed world after allowing for PPP. The issue then is, what is middle class in the developed world? This is, of course, subject to debate, but statistically it is the income level per capita per day below which the bottom third earn—with the top end of the range being the point above which the top one-third of households earn (on a per capita basis per day). As PPP is based on the USA, then clearly it has to be that range applied to the USA—and that indicates a range in US dollars and in the USA of US$49 per day per capita to US$95 per day per capita in 2012. Applying these criteria globally produces a very different result, as shown in Figure 7.8.

Basically, it raises the bar to a sensible level and means that a household that meets these criteria can have a middle-class lifestyle with reference to the standards of North America, Western Europe, and

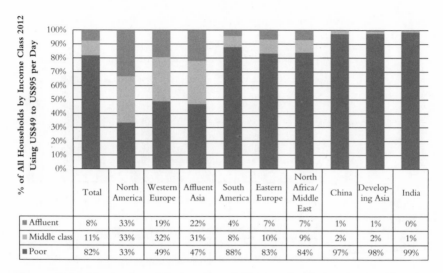

	Total	North America	Western Europe	Affluent Asia	South America	Eastern Europe	North Africa/ Middle East	China	Developing Asia	India
■ Affluent	8%	33%	19%	22%	4%	7%	7%	1%	1%	0%
■ Middle class	11%	33%	32%	31%	8%	10%	9%	2%	2%	1%
■ Poor	82%	33%	49%	47%	88%	83%	84%	97%	98%	99%

Figure 7.8   The Projected Proportion of All Households that Are Middle Class under the US$49 to US$95 Spend per Person per Day (PPP Definition)
Source: Global Demographics Ltd.

Affluent Asia. It is validated by the fact that one third of households in North America fall below and above this range.

It does not, however, dilute the argument that there is a rapidly growing middle class in the developing world. There is; the growth is rapid, it is just that the numbers are more sensible. As shown in Figure 7.9, the total number of middle class households in real 2010 values (and PPP) is projected to increase by 66 percent, from 173 million to 288 million. It is estimated that 54 percent of this increase will take place in China, 12 percent in India, 7 percent in Eastern Europe, and 6 percent in South America. So the opportunity is there, at least from a growth in the number of customers perception.

However, the sanity versus vanity issue arises again. While the growth in number

Under a more realistic definition of middle class, the total number of middle class households in real 2010 values (and PPP) is projected to increase by 66 percent, from 173 million to 288 million. It is estimated that 54 percent of this increase will take place in China, 12 percent in India.

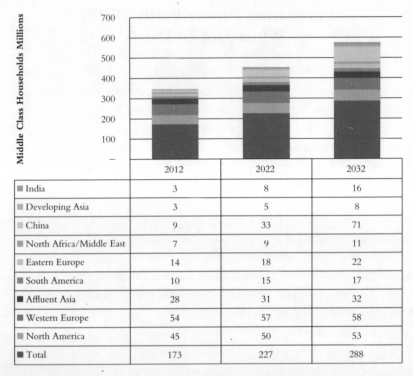

	2012	2022	2032
■ India	3	8	16
■ Developing Asia	3	5	8
■ China	9	33	71
■ North Africa/Middle East	7	9	11
■ Eastern Europe	14	18	22
■ South America	10	15	17
■ Affluent Asia	28	31	32
■ Western Europe	54	57	58
■ North America	45	50	53
■ Total	173	227	288

Figure 7.9 Projected Change in Middle Class Segment Using Higher Income Definitions
Source: Global Demographics Ltd.

of middle class households is considerable in the developing regions, their actual funds available are significantly less than those of the affluent countries. As such, while China accounts for 54 percent of the increase in middle class households, it only accounts for 25 percent of the increase in middle class incomes (the same as the three affluent regions). This is because the average middle class household in China has an income of US$15,000 versus US$61,000 in North America. (The income range for middle class is quite wide hence the difference in averages between regions.) So, while they meet the definition of middle class, they are definitely at the lower end of the income range for that definition and not really as attractive business proposition.

Purchasing Power Parity (PPP): When Not to Use It

The concept of PPP is widely used and has a sound underpinning: Essentially it is an index for the difference between two countries in total amount to be spent to achieve the same basket of goods. For example, if country A has a very low cost of living relative to country B and a country A person can buy exactly the same as a country B person at half the amount of money (using the current exchange rate) then the index would be two. Like all indices it has issues with measurement and obviously some allowance must be made for that but, broadly speaking it makes sense and is useful for understanding the affordability of lifestyles in different countries.

However, the problem is that some people use PPP to estimate market value, which is unwise. The dangers can be highlighted with a simple example. If the average Chinese urban household spends US$247 per annum on alcoholic beverages and this expenditure is then multiplied by the number of urban households then the market size is US$61 billion. This is the amount of money that will change hands using the US$ exchange rate for this year. However, some multiply that figure by the PPP index value (1.52) and say the market value is US$92 billion rather than US$61 billion. This is plainly not correct. The reader must remember that the amount of money spent is determinate; it is the value of goods received that varies. So while a person in China may buy as much beverage for US$1.00 as an American gets for US$1.52, this does *not* mean the provider of those beverages in China received 1.52 times as much revenue. In reality, in China they just earned US$1. The difference is that the price of the goods (beverage) for the person in China is (1/1.52 =) 65 percent of what it is in the United States. That means that the price of the brand being sold in China must be 65 percent of what it is in the United States, otherwise its volume (and total revenue) will be lower.

Clearly, this has significant implications. First, it means that for an international beverage brand (a tradable good) to achieve significant volume and revenue in the Chinese market it must lower its cost of production and its price to that of local manufacturers, with major implications for profit margins. Second, it means that the market value is the original figure of US$61 billion—it just requires a greater volume in China (and hence lower revenue and profit per unit) than in the United States to achieve that market value.

Strategic Implications

While this chapter has been about the distribution of incomes, the really strategic issue is one of business focus. While only 8 percent of households in the world have an income in excess of US$100,000 they nonetheless account for a very significant 48 percent of the total earned income. By 2032 it is 11 and 52 percent, respectively. Clearly this bias can be a point of concern from a sociological and fairness perspective, but it also does mean that half the earned income of the world can be reached by focusing on just 1 out of every 12 households. It is also not just about revenue. Profit margins invariably increase with the greater the value of the individual transaction, which means that the US$100,000 plus segment almost certainly accounts for over 50 percent of the profit opportunities in the world.

In 2012, an estimated 17 percent of households in China earned over US $15,000 and they account for 48 percent of the total earned incomes of households in China. By 2032, that will be 55 percent of households, and they will account for 89 percent of the earned incomes in China.

This leads to a second strategic issue. While much has been made of the rapidly growing middle class in the developing world, they none the less are almost insignificant relative to the value of the affluent market today and tomorrow. The households in China, Developing Asia, and India with an income between US$15,000 and US$100,000 account for just 6 percent of the total earned income in the countries covered in this book in 2012. In contrast, the US$100,000 plus household in North America, Western Europe, and Affluent Asia account for 44 percent. By 2032, the numbers will change, specifically to 14 percent and 42 percent, but the emphasis does not.

This does, however, lead to the third strategic issue that is the growth dynamic. The increasing affluence of China cannot be ignored. In 2012, an estimated 17 percent of households in China earn over US$15,000 and they account for 48 percent of the total earned incomes of households in China. By 2032, that will be 55 percent of households and they will account for 89 percent of the earned incomes in China. In fact it is estimated that the market value of these households will grow from an estimated US$2,004 billion to US$11,166 billion. That is 8.9 percent growth per annum. For India the numbers are significantly less attractive. While 6 percent of households have an income over US$15,000 in 2012, and this increases to 22 percent of households by 2032, in value the market is US$382 billion in 2012 growing to US$2,081 by 2032. This is 8.1 percent growth per annum, which is clearly significant in percentage terms, but is in absolute terms significantly less of an increase than that of China or the affluent regions.

Finally, attention should be given to each of Eastern Europe and South America. In the case of South America, the number of households with an income over US$15,000 will increase from 78.6 million to 114.5 million, and their market value goes from US$3,118 billion to US$5,677 billion. For Eastern Europe, the number of such households is projected to grow from 65 million to 87 million, and market value from US$2,587 billion to US$4,199 billion. Not as fast growing as China but definitely a more attractive proposition than India and more attractive than both in terms of revenue and profit potential given the higher revenue per customer. In total, their market value is projected to go from US$5,705 billion to US$9,876 billion in 2032, which is nearly as large as India and China combined, achieved on a much smaller number of households and hence higher revenue (and profit) per customer.

Summary

In this chapter we have looked in more detail at the distribution of income in society, highlighting the distribution of different income groups around the world, and how this pattern is likely to evolve over the next two decades. What we see is that the axis point for income is

US$10,000: In the years to 2032 households (and people) earning less than that amount will fall while the number of household with an income more than that amount will rise. This matters for many reasons but chiefly because this poorest group is so large accounting for 50 percent of households in 2012. The fact that this group will diminish both in absolute terms and as a proportion of the whole (34 percent) by 2032 means that, in this sense, the world is getting richer.

Those households with incomes below US$10,000 are mostly (80 percent in 2012) in Asia, and China's increasing prosperity during the next 20 years will account for most of the reduction in the size of this segment. This means that beneath the headline fall in poverty there is a sad truth: The situation in India, the Middle East, and North Africa is unlikely to change at all, with the number of households at this income level increasing very marginally (India) or rising (Middle East and North Africa). The segment of the households with incomes between US$15,000 and US$50,000 is not dominated by any one region in 2012, with Western Europe, South America, Eastern Europe, and China being the dominant regions. However, by 2032, China increases to being 31 percent of this income segment and the other three dominant regions decline in importance to this segment.

In the next 20 years, it is expected that China will increase from 3 percent to 16 percent of households with annual incomes between US$50,000 and US$100,000, while the three affluent regions (Western Europe, Affluent Asia, and North America) will reduce in proportion from 80 percent to 59 percent. Any company targeting consumers in this income segment needs to recognise the impact of these demographic changes. While China may not be important to them in 2012, it will be critical in 2032 and planning for that seismic change must happen now.

The final segment, households with incomes in excess of US$100,000, will increase in size from 8 percent of the total households (124 million) in 2012 to 11 percent (198 million) by 2032. The most dramatic change will again be in China, which is likely to grow from having 959,000 households in this segment to 17.7 million by 2032. This spectacular increase may obscure the fact that Western Europe, North America, and Affluent Asia will still hold the majority of households in this segment and, in fact, account for 58 percent of the increase in the size of this segment—and more in terms of value.

This chapter has also focused on explaining the much-used concept of the middle class. This group matters because it is increasing worldwide, particularly in Latin America and, above all, Asia, and is seen as a consumer group which spends more on higher value products and services. Crucially, the rise of the middle class is used as a basis for vital investment decisions around the world.

However, the popular perception that the middle class starts when a household earns the equivalent (after adjusting for purchasing power parity) of US$10 per person per day does warrant being challenged. Such definition means virtually all (over 96 percent) households in North America, Western Europe, and Affluent Asia are middle class, which is clearly a strange concept of middle class. Under this definition the only regions in the world where the number of so-called middle-class households can increase is all the poor areas, and hence the popular claims of a booming middle class in the developing world. The reality is that a person with the equivalent of US$10 per day to spend does not live a middle-class life by any stretch of the imagination. The conclusions drawn from such analysis in terms of range of products sought by such consumers and the profit margin per sale are seriously flawed. Often they are exacerbated by multiplying the market size by the PPP index, which is simply wrong.

If a more realistic definition is used, with the income range and associated spending power per capita per day of middle third of households in the USA (the base point for the PPP index), then a very different result is achieved. The middle income segment will be significantly smaller (in 2012 it will contain an estimated 173 million households with a US$ PPP income between US$49 and US$95 per day per capita, compared with 811 million under the more inclusive definition), but it will grow at 2.57 percent per annum and has a higher value per customer. China will account for 54 percent of this increase in households in this range, and India a further 12 percent.

Chapter 8

The Changing Pattern of Consumer Expenditure

The previous chapters of this book have demonstrated how much the core aspects of consumers can be expected to change over the next two decades. The demographic aspects, such as the changing age profile, are almost certain to happen, and the foregoing chapters have shown how dramatic that change really will be. The aspects relating to income are, of course, less certain, although there are reasonable grounds to believe the trend in affluence will be positive and, with that, households will generally have more income and, with the increased income, so too the variance in distribution of households by income will increase as outlined in the previous chapter.

The combined effects of increasing affluence and changing demographics will inevitably lead to changes in consumption patterns in each market and then collectively by region. These changes are considered to be quite significant in nature, and the purpose of this chapter is to give the reader an understanding of the potential magnitude and nature of these changes.

The reader is also reminded at this point that all financial data are expressed in real 2010 values (i.e., there is no inflation included in the forecasts) and are in US dollars using the average 2011 exchange rate.

The Basic Relationship between Consumption and Affluence

One of the greatest changes over the next two decades will be the distribution of households by income, and therefore we start this discussion on expenditure by examining how expenditure patterns differ as incomes increase. To do this it is a bit like peeling an onion. We have to start with the outer layer (gross income before tax), then gradually peel away the different layers which ultimately impact the amount a household has to spend per capita on a specific product or service category. Such is the nature of these intervening layers that two households with the same gross income (but in different countries) could end up with very different amounts to spend per capita on (say) recreation or health. However, strangely, the differences in proportion of gross income available to spend are not as great as one might expect, even after allowing for different income levels.

The first two critical layers are tax and propensity to save. Tax, unfortunately, is a given, although, of course, the rate applied does vary significantly by country, as does the progressiveness of it. Some countries have a flat rate; others have quite a steep progressive rate. Either way, this obviously reduces the amount of money that the individual household has to spend or save.

The second factor impacting on the amount a household has to spend is the propensity to save. This also varies by country and to some extent is an inverse of tax. Generally (but obviously not exclusively) the higher the tax rate of a country, the greater is the level of social services provided by the state, and the less the need for the individual (or household) to save for such essentials as health care, education, or aged care. As shown in Figure 8.1, across the regions there are differences in the proportion of

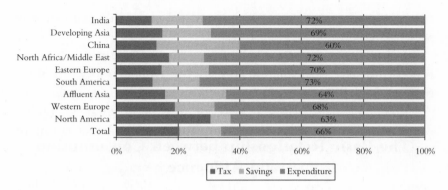

Figure 8.1 Average Proportion Allocated to Tax, Savings and Expenditure in 2012
Source: Global Demographics Ltd.

gross income that goes to each of tax and savings but the two (tax and savings) sum to a relatively equal proportion across all regions which implicitly confirms the offset between tax and need to save. On average, across all the regions/countries covered in this book, tax and saving account for 34 percent of gross income, leaving 66 percent to spend.

Of course, within each country and region the proportion that is tax and saved varies by income level, which is examined in greater detail later in this chapter, but it is perhaps interesting to note the normative pattern that exists. The normative nature is even greater if the cost of housing (rent or mortgage), health, and education is included in this initial set together with tax and savings. The reason for this is that in some economies there is a well-established mortgage industry, which means that a household can borrow to buy a home, then has the expense of paying off that loan. The reader should note that in the standard tables published by countries for their household income and expenditure surveys, mortgage is treated as an expense. This compares with those living in countries where a mortgage industry does not exist or is limited in scope or availability. In those countries, a household has to save to accumulate the capital needed to purchase the home. In some cases this involves the savings of the extended family, specifically parents. Some commentators praise these countries for their high savings rate, not appreciating that the other (typically more developed) countries are saving just as much, except that it is treated as an expense—paying the mortgage.

A similar argument exists in terms of education and health. In many countries these services are free, albeit paid for by high tax rates, so there is no need for the household to save for them.

Taking all these factors into account this produces an interesting degree of consistency across the regions. As a general rule, 50 percent of gross income goes on tax, savings, housing, health and education. The exceptions are North America where housing attracts a greater proportion of gross income, and Eastern Europe, where health is being underspent relative to tax rates and other regions of the same affluence. Figure 8.2 shows the impact of this more holistic view, and the more equal environment that exists in terms of the proportion of gross income available for other expenditure categories, specifically food, alcohol and tobacco, clothing, household operations and utilities, recreation, transport, communications, and personal care irrespective of the average income across countries/regions.

Clearly within individual countries and regions, the ability of a household to save, and how it spends the residual of its after-tax income varies by income level. At low income levels, taxes are low (or even negative in the form of social payments) as are savings. The majority of income is spent on food, housing, and clothing. As income increases typically an increasing proportion of it goes on taxes and is saved. So, as

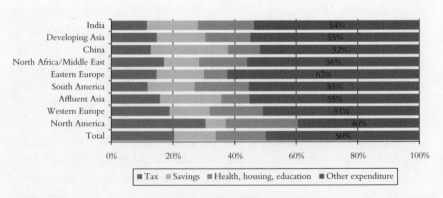

Figure 8.2 Proportion of Pretax Income Allocated to Tax, Savings, Health, Education and Housing
Source: Global Demographics Ltd.

shown in Figure 8.3, at low levels of income nearly 100 percent of income is spent on household needs. There is little or no tax and no savings. As income increases the proportion of gross income spent declines, initially quite steeply. On a global basis, the proportion the household spends then tends to sit around the 75 percent level until incomes pass US$75,000—at which point the spending declines as a proportion towards 50 percent of gross income, and conversely the proportion that goes to taxes and savings increases quite sharply. However, do note (as shown in Figure 8.3) the absolute amount spent still increases, even though as a proportion of gross income it is decreasing.

The second dynamic at play is the changing pattern of spending as the after-tax and savings income increases. In many respects this mimics Maslow's need hierarchy. At relatively low levels of income, a high proportion of total expenditure is on food, clothing, and housing. That is the survival aspect of the need hierarchy. The proportion allocated to food and clothing is, as shown in Figure 8.4, initially quite high, at 51 percent for households with an annual income below US$2,500 (especially as in countries where such households are located there are

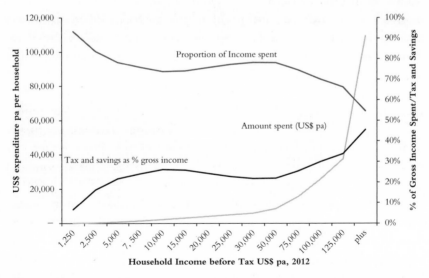

Figure 8.3   The Relationship between Gross Income, Propensity to Spend, and Absolute Amount Spent
Source: Global Demographics Ltd.

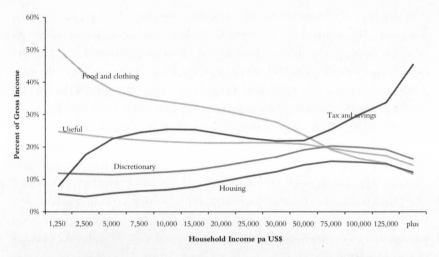

Figure 8.4 Changing Pattern of Expenditure as Income Increases
Source: Global Demographics Ltd.

generally more than three persons in the household). This declines as incomes increase and the basic needs are satisfied and other aspects of life such as education and health can be engaged in. However, on a normative basis once average household income passes US$5,000 the rate of decline slows and once again the absolute amount spent on these categories starts to increase in line with overall after-tax income. This is because the other areas of life which involve the security aspect of the need hierarchy, such as health, savings, and education, are now being met, at least to some extent. Housing, the other essential, has quite a different pattern of behaviour across the countries covered. It actually increases as a proportion (and in absolute amount) as income increases up to US$100,000, after which it starts to decline as a proportion, and grows more slowly in absolute amount.

The second category of expenditure is what we are terming *useful*. Not essential but useful to living, rather than being totally discretionary. This includes utilities (gas and power), health care, household operations, education, transport, and communications. These also collectively decline as a proportion of gross income as income increases until annual income reaches US$7,500, after which they are relatively static in share until US$100,000 is reached, when again they decline as a proportion.

The final set of expenditure categories is what is termed *discretionary*. These are the equivalent to Maslow's self-actualisation stage. They are nice to have but you can largely live without them. This includes personal care products and services, recreation, tobacco, and alcohol. These remain as a relatively low share of gross income until US$7,500 is reached, after which they increase as a proportion until US$100,000 is reached, after which they also start to decline as a proportion.

Clearly there are key trigger points in the patterns of expenditure—US$7,500 and US$100,000. Below US$7,500 households typically allocate two-thirds of their gross income to food, clothing, housing, and "useful" items. Tax, savings, and discretionary compose less than a third of their total income. At US$100,000 a different picture has emerged. Tax, savings, and discretionary typically account for 62 percent of gross income.

It is interesting to look at the relative growth rates of the different categories between these two points. This is shown in Table 8.1. While gross income increases by a factor of 13 (US$7,500 to US$100,000), food and clothing lift by a factor of 5, discretionary by 17, and housing by 25. This is important when considering the future. Clearly, then, as households increase in affluence, so the overall pattern of expenditure in a country or region can be expected to change.

However, before looking at the implications of this for future demand, it is important to consider one other phenomenon that appears to exist in the data. That is the concept of *enoughness*. It seems to apply to clothing, recreation, and personal services. After US$100,000 the

Table 8.1 Ratio of Absolute Values at US$100,000 Compared to US$7,500

	Ratio
Gross Income	13
Food and Clothing	5
Housing	24
Useful	9
Discretionary	17
Tax and Savings	10

SOURCE: Global Demographics Ltd.

proportion allocated to these categories no longer grows and, in fact, starts to decline. This suggests that even for discretionary items (just as for less discretionary items such as food, transport, communications) there comes a point where an individual simply has enough of that category. After that point the person would rather save the additional income than have (say) additional shirts, shoes, and so on. In itself an obvious scenario, but it is increasingly important as an increasing proportion of all expenditure is by households that are past this point. That could have implications for the growth in consumer demand for these categories in future.

There is the indication that "enoughness" is becoming part of consumer behaviour. The rate of growth in share of expenditure allocated to more discretionary spending flattens out and declines once US $100,000 income levels are reached. Perhaps they have enough shirts?

So what are the implications of these differences in spending patterns by income for the future levels of consumer spending in the different regions? There are two factors that drive change in expenditure patterns in a country and hence by region and overall. The first is a change in spending as a result of changing demographics (such as becoming a parent or retiring) and the second is change in spending patterns as the household increases in affluence, with the latter being the dynamics demonstrated in Figure 8.4. Changes in spending as a result of changing demographics are real, but hard to identify as they take place more slowly, and directionally are similar to that pattern resulting from increased income. As such it is not possible to isolate the effects of an ageing population on spending patterns, as they have also tended to get more affluent over the same time period. So for the subsequent analysis the key driver is how spending patterns change as a result of increasing affluence. However, the reader should keep in mind that some of that change is also to some extent a function of concurrent trends in demographics, specifically, ageing population, fewer children in the household (fewer dependents per worker), and even fewer workers per household—all of which are happening but are significantly less dramatic than the change in affluence.

First looking at the big picture, rather than by region, Figure 8.5 compares how the number of households in each segment changes over the next 20 years with how the proportion of expenditure that each segment accounts for changes over the same time period. The lowest segment (under US$15,000) increases marginally from 803 million households to 834 million—an increase of 31 million. In contrast, the income segments over US$15,000 increase in size by 9 percent, 48 percent and 60 percent, respectively. It is this increase in the absolute size of these segments that will drive the expenditure in the areas of housing and discretionary items—as well as savings.

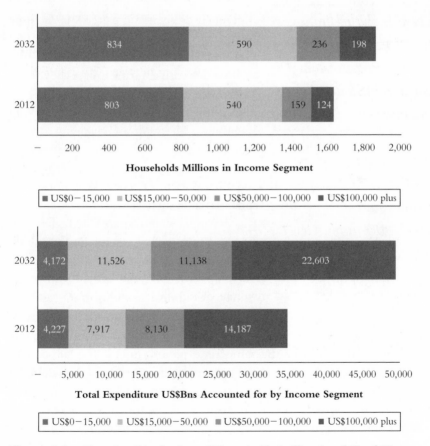

Figure 8.5 Changing Distribution of Households (millions) and Total Household Expenditure by Income Segment

Source: Global Demographics Ltd.

Obviously, the change in number of households in each income segment when multiplied by the amount they spend has significant implications for the total value of consumer market as well as the proportions accounted for by each segment. Total consumer expenditure is expected to increase from an estimated US$34 trillion in 2012 to reach US$49 trillion in 2032. That is an absolute increase of 43 percent, and represents a growth rate of 1.8 percent per annum. However, as shown in Figure 8.5, most of this increase in spending is in the income segment of US$100,000 and above. This segment accounts for 8 percent of all households in 2012 (increasing to 11 percent by 2032) and accounts for a very significant 41 percent (increasing to 46 percent) of all household expenditure in the world. They also account for 56 percent of the increase in total spending between 2012 and 2032. Hence the importance of understanding the expenditure pattern of households with an income over US$100,000.

Total consumer expenditure is expected to increase from an estimated US$34 trillion in 2012 to reach US$49 trillion in 2032.

Changes in Expenditure by Income Segment and Region

This leads to the issue of, where is the expected growth in household (consumer) spending expected to take place? Which income segments and which regions—and, of these, which offer the best profit opportunities rather than simple revenue or number of customers?

Change in Total Value of Spending

Table 8.2 shows the estimated existing and future total spending by region by income segment. Overall household expenditure is expected to increase by 43 percent over the next 20 years. In terms of growth rates by region, not surprisingly, China and India score best given the higher growth rates of household incomes and (in the case of India) number of

Table 8.2   Expected Change in Total Household Expenditure between 2012 and 2032

	US$ Bn Spend per Annum by Segment, 2012				
	US$0– 15,000	US$15,000– 50,000	US$50,000– 100,000	US$100,000 plus	Total
North America	56.9	1,102.5	2,606.2	6,225.1	9,990.7
Western Europe	133.4	1,958.7	2,800.1	4,070.7	8,962.9
Affluent Asia	61.2	832.9	1,401.2	2,826.4	5,121.8
South America	379.5	1,282.2	517.1	378.2	2,556.8
Eastern Europe	454.4	1,015.9	411.2	311.8	2,193.3
North Africa/ Middle East	236.9	280.7	140.8	254.9	913.3
China	1,444.5	887.3	137.0	56.3	2,525.1
Developing Asia	652.1	367.1	88.6	51.6	1,159.4
India	808.3	189.3	28.3	12.1	1,038.0
Total	4,227.2	7,916.5	8,130.5	14,187.2	34,461.4
	US$ Bn Spend per Annum by Segment, 2032				
	US$0– 15,000	US$15,000– 50,000	US$50,000– 100,000	US$100,000 plus	Total
North America	49.2	1,038.8	2,928.1	9,265.3	13,281.4
Western Europe	141.9	2,068.5	3,028.6	4,719.8	9,958.8
Affluent Asia	30.9	610.6	1,531.0	4,808.1	6,980.6
South America	296.8	1,739.3	1,048.8	938.1	4,023.0
Eastern Europe	328.7	1,276.9	767.3	719.1	3,092.0
North Africa/ Middle East	348.4	405.9	233.4	443.2	1,430.8
China	922.0	2,570.1	1,134.5	1,430.8	6,057.4
Developing Asia	869.0	889.4	267.7	176.3	2,202.5
India	1,184.7	926.2	199.0	102.4	2,412.3
Total	4,171.6	11,525.8	11,138.3	22,603.1	49,438.7

(*Continued*)

Table 8.2 *(Continued)*

	US$0–15,000	US$15,000–50,000	US$50,000–100,000	US$100,000 plus	Average
	Share of Market Growth by Region and Income Segment				
North America	−0.1%	−0.4%	2.1%	20.3%	22.0%
Western Europe	0.1%	0.7%	1.5%	4.3%	6.6%
Affluent Asia	−0.2%	−1.5%	0.9%	13.2%	12.4%
South America	−0.6%	3.1%	3.6%	3.7%	9.8%
Eastern Europe	−0.8%	1.7%	2.4%	2.7%	6.0%
North Africa/ Middle East	0.7%	0.8%	0.6%	1.3%	3.5%
China	−3.5%	11.2%	6.7%	9.2%	23.6%
Developing Asia	1.4%	3.5%	1.2%	0.8%	7.0%
India	2.5%	4.9%	1.1%	0.6%	9.2%
Total	−0.4%	24.1%	20.1%	56.2%	100.0%

Source: Global Demographics Ltd.

households. They are expected to grow at 4.5 percent and 4.3 percent per annum.

The US$100,000 plus households in North America and Affluent Asia, and to a lesser extent Western Europe, account for 38 percent of the real increase in total consumer spending. This compares with China accounting for 23.6 percent across all income groups.

However, the reader is reminded to look beyond headline growth rates and consider the real market value. This is shown in the third part of Table 8.2. This shows the proportion of the increase in consumer spend that is accounted for by each income segment and region. Dominant in this part of the table is the fact that the US$100,000 plus segment accounts for 56.2 percent of the increase being a reflection in the growth in the number of households in that segment as well as their average spending power. Furthermore, these affluent households in North America and Affluent Asia, and to a lesser extent Western Europe, account for 38 percent of the increase in total consumer spending.

This compares with China accounting for 24 percent of the increase in global consumer spending and India 9 percent.

China and India's growth in consumer spending takes place particularly in the US$15,000 to US$50,000 segment, although China does extend up to the top income segment as well.

Why then, given the sheer weight in number of households and people and higher growth rates, are China and India not as significant as one might expect? The answer to that lies in the oft-overlooked issue of value per customer. This of course is the "sanity" aspect of business, rather than "vanity." The average affluent household in North America, Western Europe, and Affluent Asia spends US$42,000 per capita per annum. The average household in China in that same income segment spends US$28,000 per capita. More to the point, the segment where most of China's increase takes place is US$15,000 to US$50,000 household income segment, where the average person in China spends US$5,400 per annum. The difference in the profit opportunity per customer between US$5,400 and US$42,000 is enormous.

It is also worth looking beyond the regions that tend to attract the most attention (either very affluent or very large) to some of the others. In particular South America, which, as shown earlier, is effectively becoming the middle-aged/middle-income region of the world. Its total consumer spending is projected to grow at 2.3 percent per annum, and in total it will account for 10 percent of the global increase in spending over the next 20 years with half of that being by households with an income in excess of US$50,000 per annum.

The following two subsections look at expenditure patterns by income segment and region for each of food and clothing (essentials) and discretionary items (recreation and personal care products and services) to give a contrast on how different markets might be expected to develop.

Food and Clothing   In total, households are projected to spend 50 percent more in real terms on food and clothing by 2032. As shown in Table 8.3, most of the increase in expenditure on these two categories will be in China (31 percent of total increase) driven by the significant proportion of households and population moving from a household income below US$15,000 to above that figure. India in comparison has

Table 8.3   Expected Change in Expenditure on Food and Clothing between 2012 and 2032

	US$ Bn Spend per Annum by Segment, 2012				
	US$0–15,000	US$15,000–50,000	US$50,000–100,000	US$100,000 plus	Total
North America	9.9	189.3	437.6	1,006.6	1,643.4
Western Europe	34.4	475.5	640.3	855.9	2,006.2
Affluent Asia	19.2	238.2	379.3	746.4	1,383.1
South America	204.8	605.4	218.7	143.4	1,172.3
Eastern Europe	254.9	481.4	180.1	130.3	1,046.7
North Africa/ Middle East	119.0	134.0	63.7	135.6	452.3
China	614.3	358.8	54.9	22.8	1,050.8
Developing Asia	351.8	164.9	34.5	18.0	569.1
India	351.4	59.6	6.5	2.2	419.7
Total	1,959.8	2,707.1	2,015.6	3,061.1	9,743.7

	US$ Bn Spend per Annum by Segment, 2032				
	US$0–15,000	US$15,000–50,000	US$50,000–100,000	US$100,000 plus	Total
North America	8.6	179.1	493.3	1,496.2	2,177.2
Western Europe	38.7	511.5	689.8	980.4	2,220.4
Affluent Asia	9.1	171.9	412.9	1,241.4	1,835.3
South America	162.3	825.3	436.9	340.9	1,765.4
Eastern Europe	184.5	612.1	341.1	302.1	1,439.8
North Africa/ Middle East	178.0	195.8	108.3	235.0	717.1
China	382.5	1,077.3	474.3	617.7	2,551.7
Developing Asia	459.7	403.3	106.4	62.8	1,032.2
India	486.2	290.1	46.0	18.3	840.6
Total	1,909.5	4,266.4	3,109.1	5,294.9	14,579.8

	2012 Spend per Capita per Annum				
	US$0–15,000	US$15,000–50,000	US$50,000–100,000	US$100,000 plus	Average
North America	1,075.0	2,324.9	3,706.1	7,073.6	4,681.6
Western Europe	1,394.1	3,029.2	4,841.9	8,724.5	4,869.0
Affluent Asia	1,302.6	2,836.2	5,096.4	11,412.8	5,797.8

	2012 Spend per Capita per Annum				
	US$0– 15,000	US$15,000– 50,000	US$50,000– 100,000	US$100,000 plus	Average
South America	1,156.7	2,531.6	4,919.1	9,078.3	2,460.6
Eastern Europe	1,200.6	3,157.6	6,156.4	11,672.7	2,583.2
North Africa/ Middle East	419.4	1,835.3	4,466.2	15,158.2	1,190.3
China	547.7	2,189.2	5,960.4	11,563.8	810.5
Developing Asia	453.4	1,828.3	4,398.9	8,126.9	649.6
India	309.7	1,100.8	2,213.5	3,069.6	352.0
Total	522.1	2,471.7	4,658.2	8,831.8	1,731.2

SOURCE: Global Demographics Ltd.

a much smaller proportion moving into the higher income bands, and as a result the increase in food and clothing expenditure is more moderate there, accounting for only 9 percent of the global increase.

It is also interesting to look at the per capita spend levels in 2012 by region and income segment. The range is considerable from a high of US$15,158 per capita for the affluent in North Africa and the Middle East to a low of US$309 per capita for the poor in India.

Discretionary Expenditure—Personal Care, Recreation, and Alcohol and Tobacco   In total, these categories of expenditure are projected to grow at a slower rate that the essentials which might seem counterintuitive in terms of the earlier discussion on expenditure patterns and the argument that as the number of households with an income over US$15,000 increase so will the discretionary spending grow. However, the issue that needs to be kept in mind is that the growth in discretionary expenditure is slower for households with an income in excess of US$100,000 (enoughness, as discussed earlier). This is important in this case as of the total discretionary expenditure of the regions covered; fully 54 percent of it in 2012 is by households with an annual income over US$100,000. Furthermore, it is the income range that is growing fastest in number of households.

So, as shown in Table 8.4, total expenditure on discretionary items will grow, it is by 37 percent over the next 20 years. The key growth areas are China and India, driven by the number of households and people with an income in excess of US$15,000. Unfortunately, they are just 6 percent of total discretionary expenditure in 2012, increasing to

Table 8.4 Expected Change in Expenditure on Discretionary Items between 2012 and 2032

	US$ Bn Spend per Annum by Segment, 2012				
	US$0–15,000	US$15,000–50,000	US$50,000–100,000	US$100,000 plus	Total
North America	12.8	249.6	593.1	1,413.7	2,269.3
Western Europe	28.2	449.7	680.8	1,057.0	2,215.6
Affluent Asia	15.6	237.2	450.9	997.1	1,700.8
South America	28.0	109.9	47.9	36.7	222.4
Eastern Europe	65.7	180.7	78.9	62.1	387.3
North Africa/ Middle East	18.9	24.8	15.4	28.4	87.4
China	175.4	117.3	19.6	8.3	320.6
Developing Asia	70.9	48.8	11.8	6.6	138.2
India	91.9	19.4	2.5	0.9	114.7
Total	507.3	1,437.5	1,900.9	3,610.8	7,456.5
	US$ Bn Spend per Annum by Segment, 2032				
	US$0–15,000	US$15,000–50,000	US$50,000–100,000	US$100,000 plus	Total
North America	11.1	234.1	663.7	2,100.9	3,009.7
Western Europe	29.3	475.2	751.2	1,261.4	2,517.1
Affluent Asia	8.1	171.8	479.0	1,671.3	2,330.2
South America	19.6	138.8	100.7	101.1	360.2
Eastern Europe	47.2	225.3	144.6	141.1	558.3
North Africa/ Middle East	28.5	35.7	25.4	49.7	139.4
China	106.4	317.1	145.6	209.2	778.4
Developing Asia	93.1	122.8	37.9	24.2	278.0
India	133.2	94.9	17.4	7.6	253.2
Total	476.4	1,815.8	2,365.6	5,566.6	10,224.5

| | 2012 Spend per Capita per Annum | | | |
	US$0–15,000	US$15,000–50,000	US$50,000–100,000	US$100,000 plus	Average
North America	1,389.1	3,066.0	5,023.0	9,934.9	6,464.5
Western Europe	1,140.5	2,864.5	5,148.1	10,774.5	5,377.4
Affluent Asia	1,056.6	2,824.1	6,059.5	15,245.7	7,129.5
South America	157.9	459.6	1,077.0	2,323.2	466.9
Eastern Europe	309.4	1,185.4	2,696.2	5,560.0	955.9
North Africa/ Middle East	66.6	338.9	1,076.9	3,179.2	230.1
China	156.4	715.8	2,130.8	4,189.6	247.3
Developing Asia	91.4	541.7	1,509.4	2,983.3	157.7
India	81.0	358.8	842.7	1,274.7	96.2
Total	135.1	1,312.5	4,393.2	10,417.6	1,324.8

SOURCE: Global Demographics Ltd.

13 percent by 2032 with most of the increase in share taking place in China. The fact is most discretionary expenditure is located in the affluent regions of the world, specifically North America, Western Europe, and Affluent Asia. These regions account for 83 percent of all discretionary expenditure in 2012 dropping to 77 percent by 2032, but growing in absolute amount by 28 percent and accounting for 62 percent of the total increase in discretionary expenditure across all regions over the next 20 years.

Finally, when looking at discretionary expenditure it is interesting to look at the per capita spend by region and income level. Again the differences are considerable. Households in Affluent Asia, with an income over US$100,000 spend the most per capita on this category, at US$10,000. This compares with the lowest of US$66.6 per capita by households with an income below US$7,500 in North Africa and the Middle East.

Some interesting comparisons are worth making between these two categories—food and clothing compared to discretionary items. In particular, it is worth noting that households with an annual income over US$15,000 in the three affluent regions (North America, Western

Europe, and Affluent Asia) account for 82 percent of total discretionary expenditure and 61 percent of the global increase in such expenditure over the next 20 years. This compares with the same households accounting for 51 percent of food and clothing expenditure and 25 percent of the increase over the next two decades.

The other interesting observation is in terms of affluent households in China (that is, those with a gross annual income in excess of US$50,000). This segment has, of course, the highest projected growth rate in terms of discretionary expenditure over the next 20 years. Their expenditure is expected to go from US$25.4 billion in 2012 to reach US$372 billion in 2032, clearly spectacular and driven simply by the increase in the number of households that are expected to have an income greater than US$50,000 per annum as discussed earlier in this book. However, one should keep in mind that while the growth rate is spectacular it is nonetheless a very small slice of the discretionary market. It is less than 1 percent in 2012 and reaches 4 percent in 2032. It is not enough to keep a global brand profitable on its own and they ignore other more prosperous markets at their peril.

Age Group and Expenditure—Where Should Brands Target Their Efforts in Future?

The final aspect of this examination of future expenditure levels is to look at where the growth segments are expected to be. In Chapter 2, we examined how the age profile of the population is expected to change, with the quite obvious conclusion that the older age groups are where population growth will be in future. In the previous chapter we examined how the distribution of earned incomes is expected to change, and in this case indications are that the higher income groups are likely to be the faster growing.

It is therefore useful to put these two items of information together and see the implication of these trends for expenditure patterns in the future. Partial data are available on income and expenditure patterns by age of head of household. Overall, except for the oldest age groups there is not a significant difference between the different ages of head of household segments in terms of income distribution. For the older (65+) age group the income (and hence amount available to spend) is lower. Figure 8.6 (A and B) show the global picture in terms of the aggregate amount of expenditure (vertical axis) accounted for by each age of head of household segment (front axis) and income (right side axis) segment

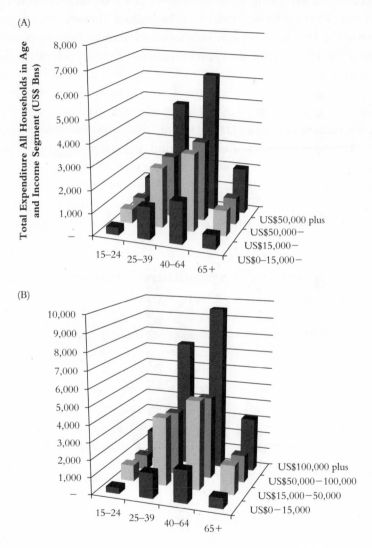

Figure 8.6 Aggregate Expenditure by Age/Household Income Segments in 2012 and 2032

Source: Global Demographics Ltd.

in each of 2012 (A) and 2032 (B), and Figure 8.7 shows the net change between those two situations.

Given that the total expenditure of all households is projected to grow from US$34 trillion in 2012 to US$49 trillion in 2032, it is not surprising that the height of the columns increase. But what is interesting is that most of the gains are in the US$15,000 and above income segments (as the bias of households is moving to higher incomes) and for persons over the age of 40 years. This is strongly demonstrated in Figure 8.7, which is the difference between the two positions shown in Figure 8.6.

This is very significant, as much has been made in recent times of the need to focus on the emerging middle-class (typically households with an income around US$10,000) as that is where the growth is. However, the numbers on a global basis do not support that conclusion. It is the older affluent segment which is the growth segment in terms of number of persons and because, by definition, they have a greater spend

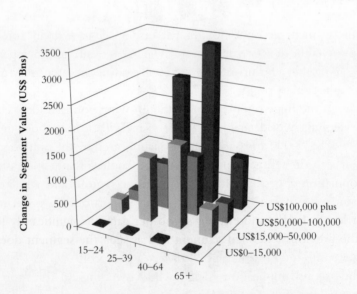

Figure 8.7   Change in Age/Household Income Segment Size between 2012 and 2032
Source: Global Demographics Ltd.

per capita, that is also the segment that dominates future consumer markets.

Of the total projected increase in consumer spending over the next 20 years, an estimated 58 percent of it is in segments over the age of 40 and with an annual income in excess of US$15,000.

Strategic Implications

The strategic implications for companies from this chapter are quite obvious and definitely counter popular claims. To achieve maximum growth in revenues, a company should focus its efforts on appealing to persons/households where the consumer is over 40 years of age and has a household income in excess of US$50,000 per annum.

Much has been made in recent times of the need to focus on the young emerging middle-class (typically households with an income around US$10,000) populations as that is where the growth is. However, the numbers on a global basis do not support that conclusion.

This segment accounts for 45 percent of all growth in consumer spending over the next two decades and 37 percent of all consumer spending in 2012. No other age/income segment will provide the same growth delta for the same time period.

Talk of the huge opportunity in the growing young middle class in the developing world (aged 25 to 39 years with a household income between US$15,000 and $50,000) is not supported by the numbers. The segment size (in terms of number of households) is not increasing as the population is getting older even in these regions and while many move into this income level a near equal proportion move out to the higher levels. Furthermore, their spend per capita is significantly lower than the previously defined segment and as such the segment does not offer the same total revenue potential let alone profit.

The second implication is that while spending on the more discretionary areas will continue to increase in total, there are indications that it may not grow as fast as might be expected for households with an income over US$100,000. It would appear that attitudes to spending are changing and savings is displacing some of the increase in discretionary spending. Discretionary spending will experience greater growth rates in the US$50,000 to US$100,000 segment than in the higher income segments. There are real indications that the affluent are reaching the point of enough.

Summary

The key conclusions flowing from this chapter have to be that even under quite conservative GDP real growth forecasts, total consumer spending in the world will continue to increase but there will be changes in the pattern of expenditure. Total consumer expenditure is expected to grow by 1.82 percent per annum for the next two decades.

With increasing affluence and hence a decrease in the proportion spent on essentials and an increase in the proportion spent on discretionary items, the expectation is the later will grow faster. That, however, will not be the case overall as the segment that dominates discretionary spending (the older affluent regions) are moving to a stage where they are saving more rather than increasing their spend on discretionary items. It is as if they have enough goods and services and would rather now save the money. In part a reflection of the current economic climate, but also probably a reflection of their age profile and concerns about funding their retirement and increasing health needs.

The consumer market is dominated, however, by the older affluent (over the age of 40 years and from a household with an income in excess of US$50,000 in real 2010 values). These persons account for 37 percent of all expenditure in 2012 increasing to 39 percent in 2032. More to the point, they account for 42 percent of the total increase in consumer spending over the next 20 years. Clearly, a brand ignores this segment at its peril.

The other useful observation from this analysis is the normative nature of expenditure across countries and regions. There is strong evidence that the offset between taxes and the provision of social services is reasonable. Countries with lower taxes have higher savings, such that after tax and savings the proportion available to spend is about the same as countries with higher taxes (and more social services). This similarity in spending proportions is greater when including housing and effectively countering the difference between saving because no mortgage is available and spending on a mortgage where they are available. The overall reality would appear to be that after providing for housing, health and education, plus taxes and overall desire to have savings the proportion available to be spent on other items is around 50 percent, irrespective of the relative level of the household income of a country.

Chapter 9

The Health Tsunami

The next issue that needs to be considered in this examination of the changing demographics and socioeconomics is the changing demand for health services. There are two aspects to this change. The first is the implications of an ageing population and the second is nature and quality of health services delivered.

It is a simple reality that the demand on health systems increases with age. The growth in such demand increases more rapidly after age 40 and, by age 64, the demand curve steepens significantly. Twenty years ago, the proportion of the global population that was or going to be over 64 years of age was small and would not have really warranted attention. However, as demonstrated quite emphatically in earlier chapters, that scenario has changed. Globally, the proportion of the population that is over 64 is currently (2012) 9 percent but this is projected to increase to 15 percent by 2032. In absolute numbers, there are an estimated 534 million persons over 64 now, and projected to increase to 970 million by 2032. That is an 81 percent increase.

Globally, the proportion of the population that is over 64 is currently (2012) 9 percent but this is projected to increase to 15 percent by 2032. In absolute numbers, there are an estimated 534 million persons over 64 now, and projected to increase to 970 million by 2032.

This increase, however, is not biased to the older affluent world. In fact, the number of 65+ persons in those regions (North America, Western Europe, and Affluent Asia) increases by only 56 percent over the next 20 years—from 173 million to 270 million. The really significant increase in the aged segment is, of course, China (with a projected 106 percent increase adding 154 million persons), then Developing Asia (adding 50 million) and India (adding 52 million). These are all countries/regions less well equipped to handle increased demand on their health system. So the story is not about the old in the affluent world, but about the old in the poor world. To put this in context, in 2012 just one in four people over the age of 64 are in China, which is in line with the proportion of the world's population it represents. However, for reasons discussed earlier, its ageing profile is more rapid, and by 2032 nearly one in three persons in the world over the age of 64 will be in China and 23 percent of its population will be over 64. Those worrying about the affluent regions not having enough workers to support their aged population should also look at China, especially as the life expectancy of China does not allow it to extend its working age in the same way as the affluent regions.

It is worth noting that the other age group that is significant in its demand on the health services, specifically 0 to 4 year olds, is not projected to grow in size globally, and in some areas, as explained earlier, where it is increasing, the rate of increase is slow. So while it will continue to be an area of demand it is not expected to be a growth area.

The other change that is expected to impact the future demand of the health sector on both government and household budgets pertains to the quality of care and availability of diagnostics and recovery rates. There is a big diversity in terms of the quality of care delivered throughout the world. While spend per person is not a definitive measure of quality, it is nonetheless a good indicator. In that respect, the differences are considerable and pressure will be placed on countries that are underdelivering to increase their spend on this category, with consequent implications for other aspects of the economy.

This chapter will now explore these two issues—trends in demand and quality—in greater detail, eventually leading to a perspective on the potential impact of this on societies.

The Relationship between Ageing and Demand for Health Services

Figure 9.1 shows the relationship between age and propensity to have type 2 diabetes for five countries; this is not atypical of the pattern across many conditions. That is, around age 35 the prevalence starts to rise and this continues at an almost linear pattern to age 70, when it flattens out. The difference between countries is the steepness of the line rather than the pattern, and the steepness can be a function of many things, including health awareness, regular exercise, diet (that affects particular conditions more than others), urban lifestyles, pollution, and diagnostics.

Given the similarity of this pattern across many conditions—both oncology as well as acute—and given that the range of conditions on

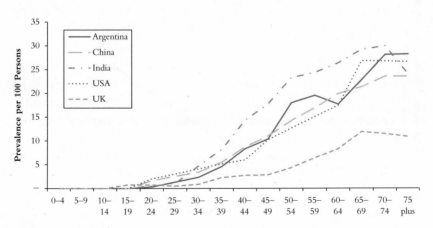

Figure 9.1   The Prevalence of Diabetes in 2012 by Age Group
Source: Global Demographics Ltd.

which epidemiology data are available varies significantly by country, it became obvious that the best approach to estimating the future demand for health care is to develop a weighted index by age for those countries for which a good range of epidemiological data were available—and apply that to all countries.

Figure 9.2 shows the pattern of prevalence for 11 conditions for a range of countries (breast cancer, colon cancer, rectum and anal cancer, lung cancer, prostate cancer, total diabetes, IGT, total hypertension, hypercholesterolemia, TB—note that the cancers have been converted to prevalence equivalents). This is the total probability of an individual of each age group having these conditions. When it passes one it means they have at least one of these and probably more. However, the value of this chart and the data are not the absolute values, but rather the relative values. The consistency in the pattern across countries means that an index can be developed for health conditions by age, then applying that to the age profile of the population can give some measure of the future demand for health services.

Figure 9.2 shows the situation in 2012. The reader should appreciate that there is some trending over time, which is not shown here.

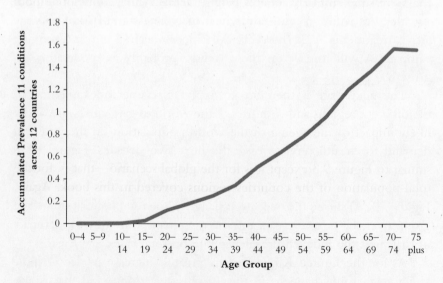

Figure 9.2 An Aggregated Prevalence Scale for a Cross Section of Countries
Source: Global Demographics Ltd.

Historical data indicate that incidence and prevalence seems to increase with urbanisation then level out or even decline (as wellness increases in acceptance). However, Figure 9.2 is a good indicator of the overall trend with age at a particular point in time.

Figure 9.3 demonstrates this process when applied to the UK, a country with an ageing population but for which even the younger age groups are growing in size as a result of high immigration impacting both birth rates as well as the number of young persons. Figure 9.3 (A) shows how the age profile of the population is expected to change over the next 20 years and Figure 9.3 (B) shows the expected total prevalence for the set of conditions used in Figure 9.2 by age group in each of 2012 and 2032.

Obviously, the biggest change is in the older age groups, where there is a combination of a high prevalence rate and a significant increase in the number of people in that age group. In total, all cases would increase from an indexed value of 36.1 million to 45.7 million. This represents a 26 percent increase in demand for treatments over the next 20 years in the United Kingdom. The reader is reminded that the mix of conditions needing treatment does vary with age, typically with the more expensive oncologic conditions increasing with age. So, the increase in cost may actually be greater than the increase in number of cases. Also the growing awareness of wellness and use of preventative treatments (e.g., the cervical cancer vaccine and antismoking campaigns) will impact on these trends, probably as moderators on growth.

The next stage is therefore to apply this same index method to the different regions and countries of the world to gain a measure of the likely impact of the ageing of the world's population on the potential demand for health services over the next two decades. Figure 9.4 is similar to Figure 9.3 except it is for the global scenario—that is, for the total population of the countries/regions covered in this book. Again, Figure 9.3 (A) shows the expected change in the total population by age group over the next 20 years and the right-hand one shows the impact of that, plus the indexed prevalence rate on total cases.

As for the United Kingdom, the greatest increase in size of individual age groups happens in the 40-plus age group, and that is also where the prevalence rate is starting to get significant, in that it passes 0.5

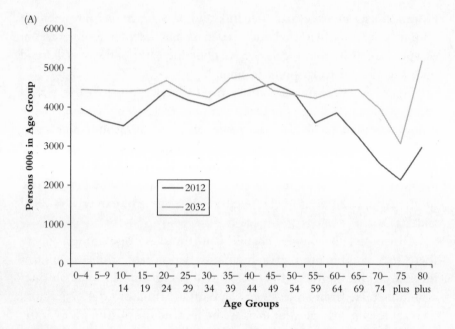

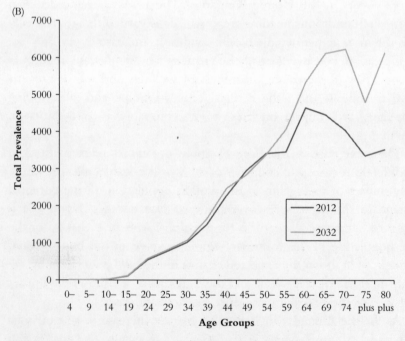

Figure 9.3   United Kingdom Example Showing the Impact in Changing Age Profile (A) on Number of Cases Requiring Treatment by Age Group (B), 2012 and 2032

Source: Global Demographics Ltd.

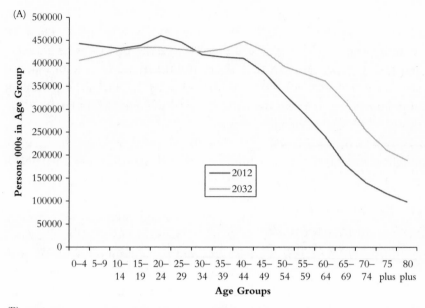

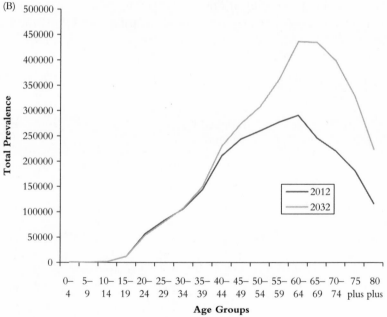

Figure 9.4   Global Impact of the Changing Age Profile on Number of Cases
Requiring Treatment by Age Group, 2012 and 2032
Source: Global Demographics Ltd.

per person (that means an individual has a 50 percent chance of having
at least one of the 11 complaints included in developing the index). As
such the impact of the increased number of older persons is heightened,
and this is shown in chart (B). There is virtually no change in indexed
number of cases for age groups under 40 years. In contrast, the number
of indexed cases increases dramatically for those over 40, and particularly
those over 50 years of age.

> *Globally, the total
> indexed number of cases
> needing treatment is
> expected to increase by 39
> percent by 2032, which is
> 1.6 percent per annum.*

The impact of this change in terms of
future potential demand on the health
services of each country/region is actually
quite considerable. As shown in Table 9.1,
the total indexed number of cases is
expected to increase by 39 percent, which
is 1.6 percent per annum to 2032. We will
examine the impact of this on total cost of
health care in the second part of this
chapter, but it is worth noting at this stage that rate of increase is not out
of line with the expected rate of increase in total real GDPs of the

Table 9.1 Indexed Number of Cases by Region 2012 and 2032 Showing
Potential Increase in Demand for Health Services

	Indexed Cases Millions pa		Absolute Increase	CAGR 2012–2032
	2012	**2032**		
Total	2,454	3,403	39%	1.6%
North America	183	245	34%	1.5%
Western Europe	252	302	20%	0.9%
Affluent Asia	145	169	17%	0.8%
South America	185	292	58%	2.3%
Eastern Europe	206	239	16%	0.7%
North Africa/Middle East	106	190	79%	3.0%
China	700	912	30%	1.3%
Developing Asia	287	460	60%	2.4%
India	390	593	52%	2.1%

SOURCE: Global Demographics Ltd.

countries/regions covered (2.12 percent per annum), suggesting that overall this increase can be afforded.

What is interesting in Table 9.1 is where the increases are expected to take place. It is not the older regions at all. In a sense Affluent Asia, Western Europe, North America, Eastern Europe, and China are already past the hump in that already the majority of their populations have moved into the age range that makes the greatest demand on health services, and subsequent increase will be slower. The countries that are under pressure are what are traditionally regarded as the younger countries, specifically India, Developing Asia, North Africa, and the Middle East, and South America. For all of these the number of persons over 40 years is starting to increase rapidly, and even while they are still a relatively small proportion of the total population they are growing to become significant. For example, in India the 40-plus age group is projected to increase from being 28 percent of the total population to 36 percent, and that is in the context of a growing total population. In absolute numbers, the 40-plus population of India increases from 336 million persons in 2012 to reach an estimated 514 million in 2032. This is a 53 percent increase in absolute number of persons. Basically, the section of their population that places the greatest demand on the health system is becoming significant and growing rapidly.

The Cost of Health Care

The second part of this analysis is to look at the impact of the projected change in demand levels as detailed in the first part of the chapter on the total cost of health care, and then overlay that with potential changes in expectations in terms of quality of delivery and the impact of that on cost.

A good overall measure of cost of health care in each country is given by the published (for all countries) share of GDP that goes on health care irrespective of who is paying (government or self pay). This total expenditure when divided by the number of persons in the country then also gives a measure of the relative quality of the delivery.

Table 9.2 summarises these two statistics. The first part shows the proportion of total GDP that goes to health care and to some extent gives a measure of the importance placed on it by the government of the countries/regions. Obviously, this does vary by country within region, but overall the variance is greater between regions than within. The range is considerable, from 17 percent for North America to a low of 3.2 percent for Developing Asia.

This difference in the proportion of GDP that is allocated to GDP is then directly reflected in the per capita spend on health care. In the North American region it is US$8,048, followed by US$4,188 for Western Europe. This compares with US$77 for Developing Asia. This is a very significant difference indeed. To some extent there is a case for making an adjustment for purchasing power parity here as a significant proportion of health care (particularly in the poorer countries) is in the form of nontradable goods (services of nurses, doctors, other hospital and health workers, etc.) and as such the lower cost of those services means greater value is delivered than indicated by a simple exchange rate conversion. For that reason, the third column shown in Table 9.2 gives the purchasing power parity equivalent. It reduces the gap, but not significantly.

Table 9.2 Proportion of GDP Allocated to Health Care and Its per Capita Value

	% Total GDP on Health	Health Spend per Capita per Annum US$	
		Raw	Adj. for PPP
Total	10.2%	1,177	1,230
North America	17.0%	8,048	8,001
Western Europe	10.7%	4,188	3,715
Affluent Asia	8.6%	3,272	2,970
South America	7.6%	792	969
Eastern Europe	6.1%	603	905
North Africa/Middle East	4.9%	361	572
China	5.1%	281	427
Developing Asia	3.2%	77	139
India	4.0%	67	151

SOURCE: Global Demographics Ltd.

Impact of Increased Number of Cases (but No Increase in Cost per Treatment) on Share of GDP Needed to Be Spent on Health

The first question to be addressed here is, what is the impact of the expected increase in number of conditions on the overall cost of health care in each region/country if there was no improvement in quality—that is treatment cost per condition remains the same? To gain an estimate of this we have taken the current total expenditure on health care in US$ billion and divided that by the indexed number of cases for 2012 to give a cost per case (third column in Table 9.3) and then multiplied that by the number of indexed cases for 2032 to give a total cost of health care for the country in that year. For example, in North America the total expenditure on health care is expected to be US$2,825 billion. There are 183 million indexed cases in 2012, which means an average cost per condition of US$15,414. This multiplied by the projected number of conditions for 2032 as shown in the fourth column of Table 9.3 (taken from Table 9.1) means that total health care costs in North America would increase to US$3,783 billion in 2032. This is a 34 percent increase in total costs. However, it represents a growth rate per annum of 1.34 percent, which is less than the projected growth of the GDP of that region—so, in total, health care costs would decline marginally as a percentage of GDP.

In fact, the projected total cost of health care for all regions covered in this book under this scenario means that overall it declines as a percentage of total GDP from 10.2 percent to 8.7 percent. Furthermore, it declines as a percentage of total GDP for all regions except North Africa and the Middle East, where it is expected to increase from 4.9 percent to 5.7 percent. So, in a sense, the impact of ageing populations and consequent increase in total conditions needing treatment does not pose a threat to the economies of the different regions. There is no apparent need to divert funds from (say) education or defense to meet the health needs of the society.

However, there is an important ingredient missing from this forecast, and that is the quality dimension. There is a huge dichotomy across the regions in the quality aspect assuming cost of treatment per case is some indicator of quality. Even after adjusting for purchasing power parity, the fact is the average Western European or Affluent Asian spends

Table 9.3 Projected Total Cost of Health Care as Driven by Projected Increase in Number of Health Conditions and No Increase/Improvement in Costs per Case

	2012			2032			Share of Total GDP	
	Total Spend on Health US$ Bn	Number of Conditions Millions	Spend per Condition US$	Number of Conditions Millions	Total Spend on Health US$ Bns		2012	2032
Total	6,576	2,454	2,679	3,403	8,542		10.2%	8.7%
North America	2,825	183	15,414	245	3,783		17.0%	16.4%
Western Europe	1,726	252	6,855	302	2,072		10.7%	11.4%
Affluent Asia	781	145	5,400	169	913		8.6%	6.8%
South America	378	185	2,040	292	595		7.6%	7.0%
Eastern Europe	244	206	1,184	239	284		6.1%	4.7%
North Africa/ Middle East	96	106	905	190	172		4.9%	5.7%
China	379	700	541	912	494		5.1%	3.1%
Developing Asia	68	287	236	460	108		3.2%	2.6%
India	80	390	205	593	122		4.0%	2.2%

SOURCE: Global Demographics Ltd.

around US$6,000 per condition; in India it is US$205 or US$463 if adjusted for purchasing power parity. Either way, there is a significant difference. Clearly, there needs to be an improvement in the quality of care in those countries spending below the average of US$2,500 per condition, which will have implications for affordability. There are two ways of looking at this. The first is what happens to cost per condition if the health-care expenditure continues its historic trend in terms of the share of GDP it represents and increases along with total GDP. The second is what share of GDP would be required if a country below the average tried to reach the current average (in real terms) cost per condition?

Impact of Assuming That Countries Maintain Health Expenditure Share of GDP on Expenditure per Condition

The impact of this scenario is shown in the last column of Table 9.4. For all but North America, Western Europe, Affluent Asia, and North Africa and the Middle East, there will be a real increase in the value spent per condition in the health system, irrespective of whether it is government paid or user paid. This clearly is desirable. The declines for North America and Western Europe are probably achievable as they spend significantly above average and there are probably efficiencies that can be realised, especially in Western Europe, given the current pressure to reduce government spending overall. The projected decline in spend per condition in North Africa and the Middle East is, of course, worrying, as the spend per condition in 2012 is already significantly below average.

However, it is impressive and encouraging that under this passive scenario China will increase spend per condition by 67 percent and India by 78 percent, under this passive forecast scenario one has to question if that really is significant. It represents an improvement in health care (assuming cost represents quality) of 2.9 percent per annum.

Impact of Assuming That by 2032 All Regions Lift to a Spend per Condition of US$1,500 or Better

This is a quality-driven estimate of the future demand on the fiscal purse of a county if it were to lift its health care quality significantly over the

Table 9.4 Impact of Trend in Share of GDP Spent on Health Projected to 2032 in Terms of Spend per Condition

	2012			2032			Increase in Real Spend per Condition 2012–2032
	Total Spend on Health US$ Bn	Number of Conditions Millions	Spend per Condition US$	Projected Spend on Health US$ Bn	Number of Conditions Millions	Spend per Condition US$	
Total	6,576	2,454	2,679	8,889	3,403	2,612	–2%
North America	2,825	183	15,414	3,479	245	14,172	–8%
Western Europe	1,726	252	6,855	1,912	302	6,327	–8%
Affluent Asia	781	145	5,400	1,126	169	6,661	23%
South America	378	185	2,040	692	292	2,372	16%
Eastern Europe	244	206	1,184	355	239	1,483	25%
North Africa/ Middle East	96	106	905	149	190	788	–13%
China	379	700	541	824	912	903	67%
Developing Asia	68	287	236	136	460	296	26%
India	80	390	205	216	593	364	78%

SOURCE: Global Demographics Ltd.

next 20 years to at least 50 percent of the current 2012 average cost per condition in Western Europe and Affluent Asia after adjusting for purchasing power parity. That is circa US$1,500 per condition before adjusting for purchasing power parity. The effect of this is shown in Table 9.5, and it is surprising in that this would appear to be largely achievable, except for Developing Asia and India. South America and Eastern Europe are already at this level so the impact on the share of total GDP that needs to be allocated to health to handle the increasing number of cases is minimal. In fact, Eastern Europe would actually be able to reduce the share.

North Africa and the Middle East would need to double the share of GDP spent on health to 9.4 percent (from 4.9 percent in 2012), but that is probably not unreasonable in that most developed countries seem to run at between 8 percent and 15 percent today.

China, with its ageing population, has been frequently subject to comment on this. Will it be able to fund its health-care system adequately, given all the older people it is acquiring over the next 20 years? The reader is reminded that the total number of persons over the age of 64 in China will increase by 154 million from its present level of 145 million. But the reality is that China is already old, so the rate of growth in number of persons over 40 (when demand on health care starts to increase rapidly) is not as fast as it has been in the past. Overall, the number of complaints will increase by a modest 30 percent relative to the rest of the world. As such the improvement in quality (i.e., lift the cost per treatment to the equivalent of US$1,500 (US$2,300 PPP in China) would mean that the proportion of GDP spent on health would need to increase from 5.1 percent as in 2012 to 8.6 percent in 2032. This is a percentage that fits comfortably with the proportion of GDP spent on health in most of the more affluent and older countries and is not out of line with what could be achieved given the government of China's desire to rebalance the society in favour of the consumer. The simple process of "socialising health care" by requiring compulsory health insurance for all staff of larger corporations (as recently introduced) will result in this increased share of GDP spent on health care becoming a reality.

The problem cases are, of course, Developing Asia and India. In both cases, to achieve that level of quality of care, while at the same time

Table 9.5 Impact on Share of GDP that Must Be Spent on Health if Require All Countries Spend at Least 50 Percent of Western Europe per Condition after Adjusting for PPP

	2012			2032			Share of Total GDP	
	Total Spend on Health US$ Bn	Number of Conditions Millions	Spend per Condition US$	Spend per Condition US$	Number of Conditions Millions	Projected Spend on Health US$ Bn	2012	2032
Total	6,576	2,454	2,679	3,219	3,403	10,954	10.2%	11.2%
North America	2,825	183	15,414	15,414	245	3,783	17.0%	16.4%
Western Europe	1,726	252	6,855	6,855	302	2,072	10.7%	11.4%
Affluent Asia	781	145	5,400	5,400	169	913	8.6%	6.8%
South America	378	185	2,040	2,040	292	595	7.6%	7.0%
Eastern Europe	244	206	1,184	1,500	239	359	6.1%	6.0%
North Africa/ Middle East	96	106	905	1,500	190	284	4.9%	9.4%
China	379	700	541	1,500	912	1,368	5.1%	8.6%
Developing Asia	68	287	236	1,500	460	690	3.2%	16.3%
India	80	390	205	1,500	593	890	4.0%	16.4%

SOURCE: Global Demographics Ltd.

absorbing an increased number of cases due to the ageing of their respective populations, they would need to increase the proportion of total GDP spent on health from its current, rather low, levels of 3.2 percent and 4.0 percent, respectively, to 16 percent, in 20 years. This is unlikely to happen.

Summary

There are really a number of perhaps surprising and unsurprising conclusions from the discussion in this chapter.

Starting with the unsurprising, finding that the total number of conditions needing health treatment will increase over the next 20 years is clearly to be expected. This is driven by an increasing proportion of the global population moving into the older (and, in this case, that is 40 years and above) age groups, where the probability of a condition occurring increases significantly.

What is surprising is that the rate of increase (and absolute increase) is highest amongst the countries that are perceived by most to be young countries. Given the bias to young people, why should they be experiencing this surge? In all cases, they had a significant lift in their total births 20 to 30 years ago and now there is a significant proportion of the population moving into what might be called the *target* zone. For example, in India, the proportion of the population that is 40 years and above increases from 29 percent to 35 percent over the next 20 years— which is significant. As a result, the total number of complaints needing attention in India will grow by a projected 52 percent; it is 60 percent for Developing Asia and 79 percent for North Africa and the Middle East. In comparison, in Affluent Asia, Western Europe, and North America, the supposedly old regions of the world with perceptions of having an emerging problem in terms of demands on the health system, the projected rate of increase in the number of conditions needing treatment is more leisurely, at 20 percent for Western Europe, 17 percent for Affluent Asia, and 34 percent for North America. China also has a low rate of increase from 2012, in that already half its population is over the age of 40. So for China the increase in number of conditions needing treatment is a projected 30 percent.

So, the pressure points are not the older countries. It is the young.

The second conclusion that is not surprising is that there is a huge difference in the current costs of treating a condition. Appreciating that the number of conditions is a notional index, it nonetheless is being applied systematically and hence the difference in cost of treatment are real. The differences are significant, with the average North American getting US$15,000 spent on each condition. This compares with just US$205 in India or US$463 if adjusted for purchasing power parity (which should be done in this case).

The conclusion that flows from this is that for all but Developing Asia and India, the other regions spending below US$1,500 (about US$2,500 in purchasing power parity terms) could increase to that level by 2032 without creating a significant stress on the overall GDP of the countries involved. While in all cases they would need to increase the share—the increase is to about 8–9 percent of total GDP—which is in line with the proportion spent by the more affluent countries.

The problem cases are Developing Asia and India. To reach that level of care they would need to allocate 16 percent of their GDP in 2032 to health care and very few countries do that, suggesting that it is probably not affordable.

So, no, there is not generally a crisis in terms of ability to fund the increasing demands on the health system as a result of the ageing populations. In fact, for the older and more affluent regions of the world the existing projected increases in total real GDP and the share allocated to health will handle the increased demands comfortably. To the extent that there is a problem, it is the inability of Developing Asia and India to lift the quality of care closer to international standard.

Chapter 10

Behind the Hype: The Future for China and India

Much is made of the rapid and welcome rise in affluence of the world's two largest countries by population: China and India. With a combined population that is 40 percent of the global total (and 45 percent of the total population of the 74 countries covered in this book) they are universally, and often superficially, seen as major markets for everything from coat hangers to nuclear power stations. More recently, China has been courted as a potential saviour of the global economy and a key player in international affairs, while India has long been regarded as a sleeping giant. Their size and impact on global population trends are just too big to ignore. Many companies and governments are understandably readjusting their policies and strategies to deal with the apparent changes and opportunities in these regions. However, there are a number of demographic factors that may impact the actual outcome over the next two decades, and this chapter explores these in more detail, to alert the reader to potential risks.

China: A Special Case

The population dynamics of China are quite unusual as a result of the one-child policy. Whereas for most countries demographic profiles change steadily, in the case of China, there are some changes taking place at a much more rapid pace as a result of this policy.

China's Changing Age Profile

It is not fully appreciated, even by those living there, that the total population of China is now static and will, after 2018, start to decline in absolute terms. This is a function of the one-child policy, which has led to a significant drop in the total number of births over the last two decades, which, in turn, is now impacting negatively the number of women of childbearing age. Obviously, as a result of this, the overall age profile of the population is becoming older; 11 percent of the total population is already over the age of 64 and this will increase to 23 percent by 2032 and with that an increase in absolute number of deaths more than offsetting the declining number of births. By 2032, the total population will have decreased to 1.297 billion from its present level of 1.348 billion and its expected peak, in 2018, of 1.357 billion. This means that there will be a reduction of 51.1 million people between 2012 and 2032, an average of 2.6 million per annum. From a commercial point of view, this fall in the number of potential customers is not necessarily a bad thing. After all, it is surely preferable to have fewer, more affluent, and better-educated people with a better quality of life than an ever-expanding, poor, and uneducated population.

There are also several important implications that flow from this change in birth rates, as well as a number of myths to explode. First is the manner in which China's age profile is changing. As Table 10.1 shows, the number of children, defined as people aged 14 years or younger, is projected to decline from 215 million to 147 million by 2032—so much for the child products and services markets in China! Even with increasing affluence, it is unlikely that profit levels from this market segment can be maintained. By 2032, a brand targeting this age group and keeping the same market share will need to have increased its price by 46 percent in real terms just to

China's population will reach a peak in 2018 before beginning an accelerating decline, largely due to the country's one-child policy. The population profile is also ageing with the proportion of people aged over 64 rising from 11 percent in 2012 to 23 percent by 2032.

maintain gross revenue (not to mention profits). The same applies to the young-adult market, which will decline from 184 million to 129 million, a drop of 30 percent. The only age segments to stay relatively stable in size or grow are those over the age of 40. In fact, China's population of people aged 65+ is projected to double in size in the next 20 years, reaching 300 million by 2032. This will be 31 percent of the total 65+ population in the 74 countries covered. Such an ageing population will undoubtedly

Table 10.1   China's Changing Population Age Profile

Age Group	Percent of Population		Persons 000s		Change 2012–2032	
	2012	2032	2012	2032	Net 000s	Percent
0 to 14	16%	11%	214.8	146.8	−68.0	−32%
15 to 24	14%	10%	184.0	129.1	−54.9	−30%
25 to 39	22%	18%	290.0	227.9	−62.1	−21%
40 to 64	38%	38%	513.8	493.5	−20.3	−4%
65 to 100	11%	23%	145.3	299.5	154.2	106%
Total	100%	100%	1,347.8	1,296.7	−51.1	−4%

SOURCE: Global Demographics Ltd.

place increased demands on the health services sector, as we discussed in
Chapter 9.

The current age profile has further implications for China's future
population growth; Figure 10.1 shows China's overall population
dynamics and highlights two significant facts. The birth rate is expected
to continue to decline as a result of the impact of increased education
and affluence, as well as an increasing proportion living in urban areas.
This will also be further impacted by the decline in the number of
women of childbearing age, as a result of fewer births 15 years ago. This
decline in number of women of childbearing age means that even if
the birth rate stabilised (or increased), the total number of births would
continue to decline, as there are fewer women of childbearing age for at
least the next 15 years until 2027 and, probably, to 2032.

The other inevitable impact is that total deaths will continue to
increase. This is not a function of any decline in the quality of the
health system, but rather a simple result of an increasingly aged population. As stated earlier, the proportion of the population over the
age of 64 increases from 11 percent to 23 percent. This inevitably
means that total deaths per annum increase and, as shown in Figure
10.1, total deaths exceed total births in 2018 and thereafter total
population is in decline.

A Shortage of Labour and Increased Wages

The next implication of China's population dynamics is the impact on
the labour force. As described in Chapter 5, when looking at labour
forces globally, China has a high proportion of its working-age population in employment, that is, people aged 15 to 64. In 2012, this is
estimated at 83 percent for males and 71 percent for females. This means
that China has no real spare capacity in its working-age population. As a
result, any decline in the size of working-age population will directly
impact the overall size of the labour force. Allowing for a marginal
decline in the propensity to be employed, reflecting better education
opportunities which will delay entry into the workforce as well as
increased affluence, which makes it possible for households to have one
parent at home, the expected decline in the working-age population
from 988 million in 2012 to 850 million in 2032 means that China's

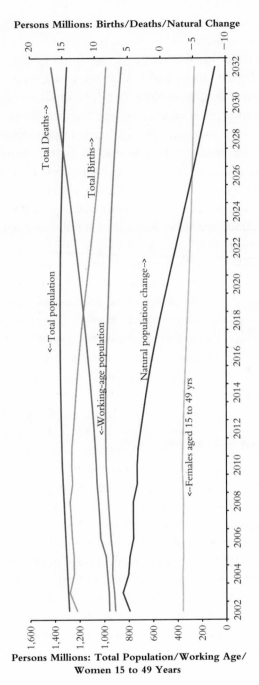

Figure 10.1 China's Population Dynamics from 2002 to 2032
Source: Global Demographics Ltd.

total labour force will also decline. The present level (in 2012) is 761 million employed persons, and this is projected to decline to 626 million by 2032. That is a 18 percent absolute decline in the size of the workforce over the next 20 years—and it is almost inevitable.

This change in size of the labour force, brought about as a result of fewer persons of working age, is very significant because the economy has benefited in the past two decades from both an increased number of workers and an increase in productivity per worker. In the last ten years there has been, on average, an additional 2.5 million workers every year entering the workforce. Now, this picture is changing. In the years to 2022, the total labour force will lose 4.7 million workers each year, and for the decade up to 2032, it will be down by a significant 8.7 million workers every year.

As a result of the looming decline in China's workforce, the country's total GDP growth will, from 2012 onwards, rely totally on increased productivity per worker rather than an increased number of workers.

As a result of the looming decline in China's workforce, the country's total GDP growth will rely entirely on raising productivity per worker. This is beneficial for Chinese workers in that it typically translates into increased real wages and household income, both of which seem likely to grow at a faster rate than total GDP. Effectively, this will increase the consumer's share of the economy. Based on the latest available data (2011), private consumption expenditure is just 33 percent of total GDP—which is very low by international standards. However, with a shortage of labour combined with increasing skill levels, and stated intention of the government to increase the consumer share of the economy, the ability of labour to gain a bigger share of the economy is enhanced. This means growth in household incomes, and this will have implications for the economy as a whole. The type and volume of consumer goods sought by this increasingly affluent population will probably exceed local production—leading to increased consumer goods imports, which could make a negative trade balance a permanent feature of the economy, with consequent implications for overall GDP growth rates.

Migration and the Rural/Urban Divide

A popular counterargument to a slower total GDP growth as a result of the decline in the total number of workers is that the younger people who move from rural to urban areas (and labour force) will experience such an increase in productivity that it will offset the decline in the total labour force. However, this assumption is not supported by the available data.

The first point is, yes, labour migration from rural to urban areas invariably did help—in the past. Available data suggest that the number of people moving from rural to urban areas has been declining significantly in the last few years. In 2004, the annual number of migrants (people moving for more than six months) from rural to urban areas was 18.6 million; by 2010 (latest actual) it had declined to 15.2 million. Furthermore, this decline is projected to continue to decline to reach 9 million in 2022 and then 6.7 million by 2032. Relative to the size of the total labour force, this migrant-worker population is, at best, 1.8 percent of the total labour force and about 3 percent of urban workers. By 2022 they are expected to be 1.2 percent of the total (about 2.2 percent of urban workers). These estimates generously assume that all migrants are employed, which, of course, they are not. It is, therefore, considered unlikely that this 1 to 2 percentage point addition to the urban workforce will result in a significant lift in productivity of the total labour force. While a contribution, it is not, and never was, hugely significant and clearly will not offset the decline in the absolute number of workers, which will be decreasing by an average of 6.7 million workers every year from 2012 to 2032.

While permanent (longer than six months) rural to urban migration was a contribution to increased productivity of the average worker, it is not, and never was, hugely significant, and clearly will not offset the decline in the absolute number of workers. Short-term migration makes no contribution to increased productivity as it largely involves unskilled labour occupations that are similar in productivity to rural work.

It is useful to understand why migration levels are slowing. Quite simply, the rural population is running out of young people. Data show that a person who turns 15 years old in rural areas, with education to lower secondary school level, has a 47 percent chance of living in an urban area within a decade and a 75 percent chance in two decades. This is because of the attraction of higher wages in urban areas, as the average urban wage is three times that of rural wages. However, the migration of the last two decades has effectively hollowed out the stock of young adults left in rural areas. Consequently, there are relatively few people left to have children and, with that, the stock of 15-year-olds to migrate will continue to reduce significantly, which is a good leading indicator of future migration numbers. It should also be noted that, historically, rural people over the age of 34 years, and particularly over the age of 39 years, have shown a very low inclination to migrate for more than six months to urban areas. This situation is unlikely to change over the next two decades so there is no basis for expecting growth or even continuation, at present levels, in rural-to-urban migration. (The reader is reminded that the one-child policy has a more liberal application for people born in rural areas where they can in various circumstances have more than one child. But it is not an issue of the number of children they can have; it is very much a function of the absolute decline in the rural areas of the number of people of childbearing age in the rural areas.)

However, while the number of rural-urban migrants may slow, the urban population will continue to grow as a proportion of the total population. This is where the young adults are increasingly located and where an increasing share and absolute number of births will take place. Conversely, as mentioned, rural areas will increasingly be populated with older persons, with consequent implications for a higher rural death rate. At present, the urban population (persons living in an urban areas for more than six months) is 52 percent of the total population and, because of these factors, it is expected to reach 62 percent by 2022 and 72 percent by 2032, helped in part by the declining total population.

China's One-Child Policy

The next issue that needs to be addressed to aid understanding of the shape of China's future is the one-child policy. There is an expectation that this will be relaxed and that it will cause a significant increase in population growth. This is also unlikely to happen. Firstly, the reality of this policy is that it applies to a minority, not the majority, of the population. It applies to ethnic Han Chinese born in an urban area (and registered as such) which, when applied, is about 38 percent of the child-bearing age population. Persons registered as rural may have more than one child under particular circumstances. What is of particular importance here is that the policy does not apply to any young people who are only children and married to another only child, which is an increasing proportion of the urban population of childbearing age. So, in effect, the one-child policy has a redundancy which is now taking place.

In terms of the rural population, which has moved to urban areas, couples can have more than one child in some situations but, unless the child is sent back to the area of the parents' registration, the parents have to pay for the child's education and health care, a situation which effectively acts as a birth constraint. This may change in the near future. That is, education and health may be provided free to migrant children as well but, this is not expected to result an increase in birth rates for reasons previously discussed.

The reality is that the one-child policy has had an impact but it is now diminishing in influence, and there is little need to change the policy. If, however, the government did relax it, the impact would probably be small. It is a well-proven, global norm that, as education and affluence increase (as they are in China), the propensity to have more than one child diminishes. If the policy was relaxed we would not expect to see a surge in births.

The reality is that China's one-child policy has had an impact, but it is now diminishing in influence. If the policy were relaxed, we would not expect to see a surge in births.

The implication of the one-child policy is that China will exhibit the following population characteristics over the next 20 years. First, the total population will stop growing, then start to decline in absolute size. Second, the population's age profile will be increasingly old, as the number of births continues to fall and life spans increase. In contrast, the remaining people of childbearing age will predominantly be urban based, so that is where the children will be. Third, the rural population will continue to decline, both in absolute numbers and as a proportion of the population and increasingly be biased to persons over the age of 40 years.

Flowing from this reality are several other issues. The first is the issue of the emergence of the childless household. As shown in Figure 10.2, already 53 percent of all households in China have no one under the age of 19 years. This is projected to reach 68 percent (two out of three households) by 2032. Why is this important? It matters because it represents a consumer segment with a particularly high propensity to consume, the Working-Age Empty Nester. In China, these households consist of two adults aged 40 to 64 years. They have their own apartment and, if urban, it is well-equipped with a television, washing machine, and other items, with no dependent child in the household. (Twenty years ago they tended to get married quite young and have the one child quite quickly.) This household's level of disposable income (after deducting items such as food, clothing, and housing costs) is significantly higher than it is for those with a child, who are generally younger and bearing the costs of a child.

The simple process of moving from a three-person (with 1.7 earners) household to a two-person (with 1.7 earners) household has a significant impact on per capita income. Taking the average urban household income in 2012 as RMB (renminbi) 86,652 before tax, this translates into a before-tax income of RMB43,326 (US$6,800) per capita for the childless household, compared with RMB28,898 (US$4,500) for

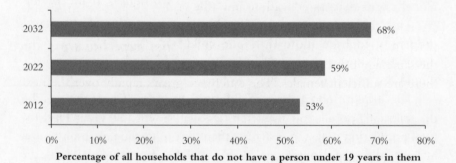

Percentage of all households that do not have a person under 19 years in them

Figure 10.2 Percent of All Households in China that Do Not Have a Person Less than 19 Years Old
Source: Global Demographics Ltd.

the household with one child. That is a significant (50 percent) difference. What this means is in these empty-nester households, an increasing proportion of money is available for discretionary items such as better-quality, healthier food, personal-care products, health-maintenance expenditure (i.e., gym membership), transport, and recreation. It is little wonder, then, that the markets for these items have grown in the last few years and are expected to continue to do so in the immediate future. The number of working-age, empty-nester households is projected to increase from 232 million in 2012 to 290 million in 2032, accompanied by an average of 4.9 percent per annum increase in real before-tax urban household incomes.

> *53 percent of all households in China have no one under the age of 19, and this will reach 68 percent by 2032. This matters because it represents a consumer segment with a particularly high propensity to consume.*

The Gender Bias

The other side effect of the one-child policy is quite a serious and growing bias in gender of births. Based on age-profile data published by gender, it is possible to derive the gender bias of live births in earlier years. This is indicating 1.25 males to every female, with no indication of a declining trend, even as more people become aware of the potential issues of too many males.

The impact of this is mainly in terms of the ability of marriageable age males (defined in this instance as 25 to 39 years) being able to find a wife. At present, the problem is not too bad. Assuming they marry into the same age band (typically one to two years younger) then, in 2012, there are sufficient females. The difference grows rapidly over the next two decades. By 2022, the shortage is 22 million females, and 15 percent (nearly one in seven) marriageable age males will not be able to get married. By 2032, the gap will be 40 million, and 24 percent (nearly one in four) of males who turned 25 after 2012 would not be able to get married to a girl of a similar age. The problem could be reduced by marrying ever younger girls (to age 18) but that will at best halve it. This will inevitably create social problems.

Household Income and Expenditure in China

So, what does this mean for household incomes and spending patterns? First, the reader should review the subsection in Chapter 6 entitled "How Fast Can China's GDP and Household Incomes Really Grow?" Household income is such an important point that we need to revisit the data to highlight exactly what it means for China. As we saw, there is a simple way to gain a reliable estimate of the before-tax household income. This starts with the household private consumption expenditure component of GDP. This is a fairly reliable, independent measure of the total expenditure of all households, irrespective of whether the income behind that expenditure has been declared for tax purposes. By dividing this figure by the total number of households, we get a quite reliable measure of the average expenditure per household. This is a very effective base point from which to work. In the case of China, the private consumption expenditure component of GDP is available separately for both the urban and rural economies of each province.

We can then use data from the household income and expenditure survey (which has been produced annually since 1984 with sample sizes now in excess of 150,000 and using professional survey methods) to estimate with some confidence what proportion of disposable income (after tax) this expenditure is and then, what the after-tax disposable income must be. By applying the inverse of the tax tables, we are then able to determine pretax income. Finally, using the data from the household income and expenditure survey on the distribution around the mean, we are able to determine the overall pattern of households by income before tax, which gives the known level of average expenditure per household. The result of this analysis for 2012 is shown in Figure 10.3.

What is evident from this chart is that the segments earning over US$15,000 before tax (about RMB100,000) are urban based but are currently a small proportion of all urban households, being 35 percent of the total. We call this segment the *consumption class*, as it is typically the income point at which some discretionary spending takes place, including overseas holidays, purchase of luxury brands and the like. While it is a small proportion of urban households, it is nonetheless 78 million households and, in terms of total urban household expenditure in China, this segment accounts for 58 percent of urban household expenditure and

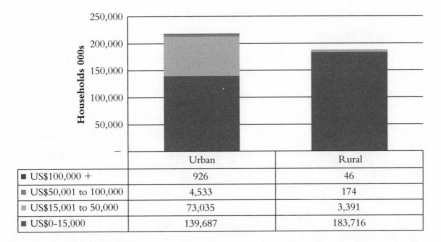

	Urban	Rural
■ US$100,000 +	926	46
■ US$50,001 to 100,000	4,533	174
■ US$15,001 to 50,000	73,035	3,391
■ US$0–15,000	139,687	183,716

Figure 10.3 Distribution of Urban and Rural Households by Annual Before-Tax Income (2012)
Source: Global Demographics Ltd.

46 percent of all—urban and rural—households' expenditure). What is less clear is how this segment will grow. The future for the consumption class will be largely determined by what happens both to total GDP and to the proportion of it that reaches the consumer (i.e., household private consumption expenditure).

There is good reason to expect that total real GDP will grow, probably by an average of 3.4 percent per annum over the next two decades (averaging 4.1 percent per annum for the decade to 2022). This figure is derived from projected trends in the education profile of the workforce, and how this will affect productivity per worker, as well as taking into account the declining number of workers. However, while that rate of growth is good, even enviable, it is possible that household incomes will grow even faster. As mentioned earlier, GDP is not the same as consumer spending. The consumer spend is a subset that is reported as the household share of PCE (private consumption expenditure). In China, this has declined as a proportion of the economy in the last decade. Consumer spending as a proportion of total GDP is now very low by international standards at 33 percent (in 2011, the latest actual published), down from 43 percent in 2002 and the government now intends to increase this. It means that the workers' share of the economy is likely to increase. To what figure is debatable but, if it reached 40 percent by 2032, then real wages would increase by 6.27 percent per annum in real terms (household incomes would also rise but at a slower rate of 5.4 percent per annum due to the declining number of workers per household, from 1.9 to 1.6). These numbers compare with 3.4 percent per annum for the total real GDP over the same period.

In the years to 2032 this will have a significant impact on the distribution of households by income, as shown in Figure 10.4. The affluent segment in today's terms is projected to increase significantly in absolute size and, consequently, this will have a considerable effect on consumer spending and retail sales—and, of course, on the range of items being sought.

In the 20 years to 2032, the absolute number of urban households with an income in excess of US$15,000 per annum will rise from 78 million to 198 million. In short, even under this relatively conservative GDP real growth scenario, China is projected to add an average of 6 million urban households every year to the consumption group. The impact of this increase in the demand for products other than the basics is going to be enormous and will, potentially, move China from being a country where other nations go to buy things from (*manufacturer*) to a country where people go to sell goods (*consumer*). Of course, this will have an effect on total GDP in the trade balance, which may become negative and slow the economy's growth even further.

The reader should also note the change in the relative number of urban and rural households over time. Total rural households are

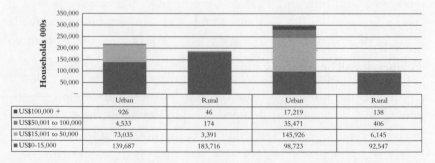

	Urban	Rural	Urban	Rural
■ US$100,000 +	926	46	17,219	138
■ US$50,001 to 100,000	4,533	174	35,471	406
■ US$15,001 to 50,000	73,035	3,391	145,926	6,145
■ US$0–15,000	139,687	183,716	98,723	92,547

Figure 10.4   Projected Change in the Distribution of Households by Income (2012 to 2032) in Real US$ Using 2011 Average Exchange Rate and 2010 Values
Source: Global Demographics Ltd.

projected to decline from 187 million to 99 million—mainly as a result of older persons dying, although, of course, also a function of the continuing but slowing urban migration.

Finally, it is important to look at the distribution of earning power within China. There are grounds for treating China as 31 countries (27 provinces and 4 municipalities). Some companies already do this when developing their investment priorities. But, when considering the affluent "consumption class" (i.e., households with a real income before tax of US$25,000 and above), it actually pays to focus on cities. Of the 862 cities with more than 200,000 urban residents in 2012, 64 account for 75 percent of all such households—with the smallest of these 64 cities containing 50,000 "consumption" households. Such is the concentration of wealth in China. By 2032 the top 210 cities will account for 69 percent of them—with the smallest of these having 100,000 such households in it. So clearly the affluence will spread, but indications are that it remains relatively concentrated.

Of the 862 cities with more than 200,000 urban residents in 2012, 64 account for 75 percent of all urban households with an annual pretax income in excess of US$25,000.

The Future for India

Given the changes taking place in China's economy and the, probably, inevitable slowing of its economic growth, many businesses are now turning their attention to India. In fact, many people assume that because India has a very large population with relatively low household incomes, it will be another China, leveraging its large, cheap labour force to achieve rapid economic development. However, it is unlikely that this will be the case, as India has very little similarity to China on any dimension other than population size.

One of the most fundamental differences between China and India is in their

One of the most fundamental differences between China and India is in their age profiles.

age profiles, as shown in Figure 10.5. As a result, India has a totally different consumer, household, and labour force environment, placing it on a completely different trajectory. For example, even though India has a smaller total population than China, it nonetheless has 152 million more people aged 0 to 14 years than China. It is a child market, whereas China is an older adult market. It also impacts on its productive power. 73 percent of China's population is of working age, compared with 63 percent of India's—a difference of 323 million potential workers. As we have seen previously, age profile matters as it affects many issues, from future population growth, labour force growth and size and spending patterns, to demands on the health and education sectors.

This difference is a function of the relatively high rate of births in India. India has not been particularly effective in limiting the number of births in the past decade. In recent times, it has managed to lower the overall propensity of women of childbearing age to have children—although, at 83 per thousand females of childbearing age, it is still high by world standards. The global average is 62 and most developed countries are at levels below 60. As a result, there have continued to be a significant number of births over the previous two decades and, consequently, the number of women of childbearing age will continue to increase for the next 20 years (most of the new entrants into this group are already alive, so it is a reliable forecast). This more than offsets the projected continued decline in propensity to have children from 83 per

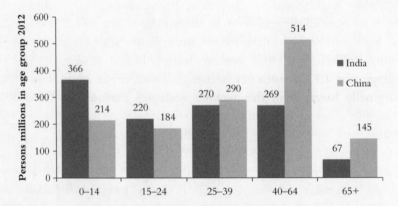

Figure 10.5 Comparison of Age Distribution in India and China in 2012
Source: Global Demographics Ltd.

thousand in 2012 to 63 per thousand in 2032. The net effect is that India is projected to produce 25 million babies every year for the next 20 years. This compares with China, which in 2012 is projected to have 13 million births—and this is expected to decline to 8 million by 2032. This difference is significant, as children are expensive from a societal as well as household point of view.

India's Demographic Profile

Figure 10.6 shows the population dynamics of India from 2002 to 2032. While deaths are increasing they are relatively small in number, reflecting the fact that the overall population remains youthful. While the number of women of childbearing age continues to increase, it is at a slowing rate, and that (combined with a declining propensity to have children) means that the total number of births will begin to decline after 2019 and total population growth also starts to slow.

At the same time, another dynamic comes into play: the movement of the population into working age and, hopefully, employment. The proportion of the population that is of working age is expected to increase from 63 percent in 2012 to 67 percent by 2032. With the trend in the propensity for these people to be employed set to increase marginally, the number of people supported by each worker (including themselves) will decline from 2.72 to 2.61. While this is still high by international norms, it is a move in the right direction.

As we highlighted in Chapter 4, India's young age profile means there are marked differences in household size, number of households, and household composition from China. India, with a large number of young children, has a high average household size. In fact, in 2012 the average was 4.73 persons per household, with urban households being marginally lower than the average with 4.3 persons per household. Also, the average household size is not expected to change significantly over the next 20 years, with the overall average becoming marginally lower, at 4.64 by 2032 (down from 4.73 in 2012). Therefore, even though India's total population of 1.1 billion people is not dissimilar to that of China, India has significantly fewer households with more people per household. The estimated number of Indian households in 2012 is 252 million (compared with 433

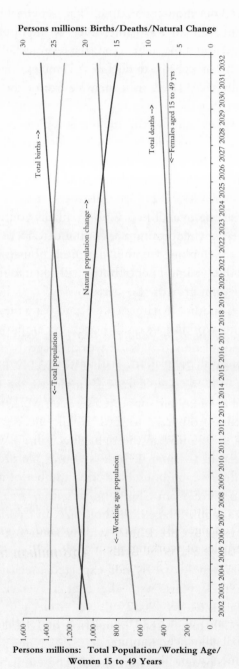

Figure 10.6 India's Population Dynamics from 2002 to 2031
Source: Global Demographics Ltd.

million for China). This matters because the household is where consumption decisions are made, and the profile of the household will impact spending patterns.

The great majority of these households (84 percent) will have at least one, but typically two, children under the age of 19, which has important implications for the demands placed on the income earned by each household. Quite simply, the higher household size in India means that the average household has much less to spend per capita than those in China. The average household income for India is US$5,724 per annum and the average household size is 4.74, giving a per capita income of US$1,207. This compares with a US$9,674 average household income in China, which, divided by an average household size of 3.11, gives a per capita income of US$3,110. This is a significant difference affecting the ability of each household to save and to engage in discretionary expenditure (including on education and health).

India's Labour Force, Education, and the Prospects for Growth

India's large and youthful population, with 50 percent of its people under the age of 25, means that the labour force will grow in size over the next two decades. If one uses the trend in the current propensity of people aged 15 to 64 to be employed, along with the projected number of people of that age group, then the labour force will grow from 438 million in 2012 and, by 2032, it will reach 554 million—a substantial (26 percent) increase.

Importantly, however, the workforce could be much larger if attitudes towards female participation change. At present, just 39 percent of females of working age are employed (compared with 75 percent of males). If this were to increase, then India's total labour force would grow very rapidly indeed—and, with that, total earnings and individual affluence, assuming that there is employment available.

India's labour force is projected to grow from 438 million in 2012 and to reach 554 million by 2032—a substantial (26 percent) increase.

However, observing other countries where there is low female unemployment, it would suggest that this situation does not change significantly over time, even if there is an improvement in the educational standard of females. Malaysia is a case in point where there has been no significant increase in female participation rates over the last decade in spite of having a very good education standard for females. This means that the average household in India has more people in it than China, but it also has fewer wage earners. The average for India is 1.7 wage earners in a household of 4.9 people. This compares unfavourably with China, where there are 1.9 wage earners in a household of 3.11 people.

While social attitudes are probably the main constraint on female employment in India, this is exacerbated by inequalities in educational opportunities. Females are significantly less likely to be educated than males and, overall, in 2012 only four out of five children receive basic primary education, a scenario which has serious implications for India's ability to sustain economic growth. In fact, the single most important issue determining India's future is the question of whether it can improve access to, and the quality of, its education system. India's less-than-universal education system has implications for the future of its labour force, birth rates, and household size and spending, as well as urbanisation.

Looking at the educational profile of the adult population (and by implication the labour force), while it is globally competitive in terms of the proportion of people with a vocational or tertiary qualification, it is underrepresented in terms of the number of people that have either partially or completely received a secondary education. As these are the people who provide middle management and skilled labour, this deficiency constrains the ability of the economy to grow. In fact, if the education standard is not improved it will mean that India can only offer a very large, but unskilled and cheap, labour force, as it will be dominated by those with only a primary education or even less. While this may enable it to be cost-competitive in low-skilled manufacturing relative to other places in Developing Asia, and particularly in China, we should also keep in mind the continual advances in manufacturing. For example, robotics is already replacing low-skilled jobs in much of the developed world, with robots working 24/7 and, ultimately, being cheaper as well. As a result, in 20 years' time India's demographic dividend may actually be a large mass of unemployed people—a demographic time bomb that is already ticking!

However, the good news is that the education profile is improving, and if the trend in enrolments by age continues and this plays through to the education profile of the labour force, then this will help significantly. Figure 10.7 shows the estimated education profile of the adult population of India in 2012 and 2032, after taking into account these trends. The improvement—particularly in respect of secondary educated persons—is significant in percentage terms (and even more impressive in numbers of people), which is a positive scenario for India. However, the same chart shows China's profile in 2012, and the bad news is that it takes India 20 years before it catches up with where China is today in terms of labour force skill profile.

Furthermore, India's less-than-universal educational standards have implications for urbanisation. Invariably, the education opportunities are fewer in rural areas and, as a result, the ability (let alone the desire) to move from agricultural employment to higher-paid and more productive urban employment is constrained, particularly for those with no education. This is one reason why education is the key variable for India's future. The lack of education restricts mobility of labour and, as a

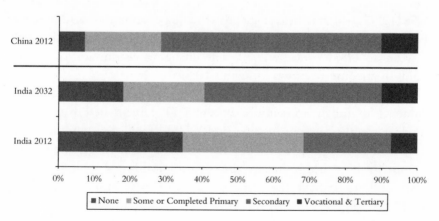

Figure 10.7   Education Profile of Adults in India 2012 and 2032 and China 2012

Source: Global Demographics Ltd.

result, urban population growth is substantially a function of overall population growth, rather than resulting from the movement to urban areas and jobs. The proportion of the population that is urban has changed very little in the last decade. However, with the current trend in the availability of education, we expect that to change in the future. In 2012 it is estimated at 30 percent of the total population, and by 2032 it could reach 39 percent. Essentially, the improved education profile will enable India to move an increasing proportion of its population from lower-paid rural jobs to more-productive jobs in urban areas, which would help raise the living standards of some of its population.

Clearly, India's GDP is expected to grow, driven by the assumption that the growing labour force will continue to be employed at the present rate. If one also assumes that the historic relationship between the labour force's education profile and productivity per worker continues and is positive, then India's total GDP will increase at an average rate of 5.17 percent per annum for the next two decades. The private consumption expenditure component of GDP in India is 57 percent, which is low by international standards, but significantly higher than China, and there is reason to expect this to decline marginally over the next two decades as there will be little pressure on wages due to the additional 6 million persons a year looking for work. Based on this, it is estimated that the average household income, taking into account the number of workers per household, will increase from US$5,724 to US$11,892, which is an average growth rate per annum of 3.72 percent. For urban households, the average is US$9,079 in 2012, which will increase to US$17,906 by 2032. The changing distribution of households by income is shown in Figure 10.8.

The data suggests that there will be a significant increase in the affluence of urban households. Whereas 71 percent of urban households currently have an income under US$10,000 per annum, this is projected to decrease to 37 percent by 2032 raising significantly the number of households that are above this point. Rural areas, however, will continue to have the majority of households earning below the US$10,000 figure.

Finally, it must also be remembered that this average household income has to be shared across just over 4 persons, if urban, and nearly 5 if rural. This means that in 2012 the average urban person is living on

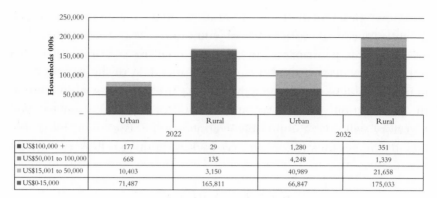

	Urban	Rural	Urban	Rural
	2022		2032	
■ US$100,000 +	177	29	1,280	351
■ US$50,001 to 100,000	668	135	4,248	1,339
■ US$15,001 to 50,000	10,403	3,150	40,989	21,658
■ US$0-15,000	71,487	165,811	66,847	175,033

Figure 10.8   Distribution of Households by Income in India
Source: Global Demographics Ltd.

US$5.71 per day, increasing to US$11.56 over the next 20 years. For the average rural dweller, the per capita income per day is US$2.27, increasing to US$4.76 by 2032. Under this scenario, it does not matter what one assumes about the cost of living: The reality is that the average household has very little room to save. In 2012, it is estimated that the average urban household saves US$1,686 per annum and the average rural household saves US$580 per annum. It means that there is, on average, little room for discretionary expenditure for the average household (as discussed in Chapter 8) but, more to the point, in the context of this chapter when multiplied by the number of households, this gives an estimated total for annual domestic savings throughout India in 2012 of US$238 billion. While that is a large sum of money, it is much less significant when compared with the same figure for China, US$744 billion. It means India's ability to invest in its own development is significantly less than China's. This is why improving education in India is so important. Without that, India will not increase in affluence or, more importantly, reduce birth rates. Until they do, the average family will have too many dependents relative to its income and will not be able to save. As a result, the actual development of the country, including its infrastructure, will inevitably be curtailed.

India's present position clearly highlights the complex interplay between demographic realities, economic development, social norms and politics. As we saw in earlier chapters, for India to sustain its economic progress and, by implication, remain politically stable, it urgently needs to raise levels of educational attainment, encourage greater female participation in the workforce (or find another way to improve productivity) and increase state spending on health care. It is tempting to think that leaving these things undone will merely result in the preservation of the status quo, but it won't. India's sheer size and trajectory will slow and possibly even jeopardise its growth. Either the country moves forward or it moves backward; there is no standing still.

Strategic Implications

There is one overriding strategic implication that flows from this chapter, and that is that companies need to have quite different strategies for these two very large but relatively poor markets. In fact, for many companies the differences in the stage of demographic development of the two mean that, whereas one country is a great opportunity for their product or service, the other is not. Children's products and discretionary services are cases in point.

The two countries also differ significantly in terms of their developmental capability. The reality is that China (significantly as a function of the one-child policy) developed an effective education system, such that it is now in a position where compulsory education for all six to 12 year olds is a reality (and has been for some time). As a consequence the capability and mobility of its labour force increased significantly. It is, therefore, possible to build factories or offices in China and be reasonably assured of staffing them with the appropriately skilled people. Such is not the case for India. While it is competitive in terms of highly skilled staff, it cannot deliver in the middle skill level, and will not be able to do so for 10 to 15 years. This makes it less attractive as a manufacturing location for anything but the most basic of products, with consequent implications for *productivity* (value of what is produced).

Next, for both countries there are demographic/socioeconomic factors that create potential political risk. In China, it is the disaffected young male who simply cannot form a household and become part of the normative community. In the case of India there is the real risk that the relatively unskilled labour force will be replaced by robots in other parts of the world, thereby creating significant levels of unemployment. Both risks are real, with India's perhaps being the more likely of the two to cause investment risk.

Summary

Perceptions of China and India are changing fast, and this will continue with highly significant economic and political consequences.

China's challenges include sustaining economic growth at a time when the population is ageing and there is a steepening decline in the size of its workforce. In this situation, the country's GDP growth will rely on increased productivity per worker. This is good for Chinese workers, because it will translate into increased wages and household income, with both likely to grow at a faster rate than total GDP. Delivering increases in productivity is one of the main challenges for the Chinese government. Furthermore, the political imperative of the need to sustain economic growth rates to maintain full employment ceases to apply. Instead, the focus will be on sustaining per capita economic growth to meet the rising expectations and aspirations of the new consumption class.

Although its progress has also been phenomenal over the last two decades, India's economic challenges are now altogether greater than China's. At the heart of India's future lies the need to improve education for a vast number of current and future children. The workforce needs to be more mobile, better skilled, more productive, and less inclined to have children. All of these issues are profoundly influenced by education. Failure to achieve these improvements in the next two decades, if not the next decade, could have very significant social (and, by implication, political) consequences.

Chapter 11

Conclusion

The objective of this, the final chapter, is to help the reader form an understanding of the overall nature of how the world might change over the next 20 years in terms of its demographic and socioeconomic profile. The preceding chapters have given a lot of data and information about specific aspects of the changes that will take place. This chapter will try to bring it together into a single, more easily assimilated, description for each region.

Throughout this book we have used nine groups by which to summarise the 74 countries included in the database that underlies this book. This has been done to help keep the discussion to manageable proportions. Analysis has shown that the variance between these regions is greater than the variance within them, and thus it is a reasonable approach to use. However, the reader is reminded that there is variance within the regions as well. In addition, two of these regions are single countries, China and India. It is necessary to treat them separately because they are so large in terms of population. What happens in either demographically will have significant implications for the rest of the world.

The Old Affluent Regions

Starting first with the older affluent regions, it is important to appreciate how significant they are to the overall consumer markets of the world. In absolute amount spent by households these regions account for a staggering $0.70 out of every US$1 spent in the world. Clearly, whatever happens to the consumer markets in these parts of the world has very significant implications for the rest of the world, if for no other reason than they buy the production of the factories elsewhere in the world and therefore provide significant employment and well-being. What is more, they account for this $0.70 out of every dollar spent, even though they contain only 18 percent of the population of the countries covered, which means that the spend per household (and profit margin) is significantly higher than any other region. The average spend per capita per annum of the old affluent regions is US$24,000, compared with an average for the globe of US$6,100.

The importance of these regions as a consumer market is disputed by some because they tend to either modify the data of other regions using purchasing power and thereby makes this older affluent region appear less important, or they use total GDP as a basis of comparison, which is not appropriate for consumer market size analysis. It is quite incorrect to use purchasing power parity (PPP) in this manner. Purchasing power parity is a measure of the relative amount of money required to get the same goods and services in different countries. So, while someone in India may get for $3 the same goods as a person in North America will get for $10, it does not change the fact that in both cases the amount of money spent is US$3 and US$10, respectively. The difference is that the goods the individual in India receives cost one-third of that which the person in North America pays. The value of the market is the price paid for the goods ($3 and $10, respectively) and that does not change. Clearly the profit margin on the goods sold for $3 is much lower, perhaps justified if the volume is there. However, many international brands cannot produce at that price and make a profit or avoid arbitrage damaging their brand/margins elsewhere.

The second important aspect of the spending power of these affluent regions is the growth of it. In recent years, perhaps encouraged by the investment industry where growth rate is a significant indicator of their own success, there has been a focus on those growth rates rather than absolute increases in value. This can lead to adopting investment strategies that may not be the wisest. To explain, in total, for the 74 countries covered in the book, household expenditure is projected to increase by 3 percent in absolute real (no inflation) terms over the next 20 years, which represents 1.82 percent per annum annual average growth rate. Of this US$14,977 billion increase in consumer expenditure, 41 percent of it is accounted for by these three older affluent regions with just 18 percent of households. Any company or investor that is not targeting these regions significantly is effectively missing out on just under three-quarters of consumer spending and nearly half the future growth in that spending. And yet so many commentators talk about the demise of the traditional consumer markets.

It might also pay at this point to reinforce just how important the affluent portion of these regions is—that is, focusing on just households earning over US$100,000 in these three regions. In 2012, they represent 38 percent of all consumer expenditure in the countries covered in this book and account for 39 percent of the projected increase in consumer expenditure globally. The luxury market is alive and well in these consumer regions. Furthermore, the older affluent regions account for 92 percent of all expenditure by all households with an income over US$100,000 across all countries, which reduce to 83 percent by 2032.

However, these commentators may not be too far off the mark when they talk about the demise of the traditional markets, except in reality, the demise is a function of the change in the nature of the consumer in these markets rather than lack of money. There are two significant changes taking place in these regions. The first is in respect to the proportion of the population still earning money. The expectation of many was that the labour force in these countries would start to shrink in absolute if not relative size as the populations got older and a greater proportion had retired. However, the nutritional and health history of the populations in these regions is such that adults of age 50 today typically have a life expectancy of around age 80. Furthermore, at age 60 they are still physically and intellectually capable, and this continues for many well into their 70s. That, combined with the need to finance as much as 20 years of life after age 60, means that a very high proportion of these people are staying in the workforce. Their role may change, as may their earnings, but the point remains that a significant proportion are still employed and therefore still earning money, giving them additional consumption power. It also means the overall economy effectively gains extra engines. Japan is the classic example of this scenario. Many commentators have claimed that it will have problems because of its ageing population and fewer workers to support them. The reality is that its existing labour force of 62 million will shrink by a mere 3.8 million in the next 20 years. Furthermore, the number of dependents per worker does not increase (and is one of the lowest in the world) and there is not an immediate problem of not being able to care for its ageing population. This is typical of virtually every country falling in these three regions.

This means that overall household incomes are sustained, and actually grow. The growth rates again might appear miserly (approximately 1 percent per annum) compared with other parts of the world but the reader is reminded of the following. First of all, the focus is on households with an average household income of around US$95,000 per annum. A 1 percent increase in that is an extra US$950, for a household of two-and-a-half people. (Already over half the households in this region have no children.) That compares with China, with 5.67 percent growth of an average urban household income of US$9,700, which is an additional US$548 for a household of 3.1 persons. So, in absolute terms, the slow-growth affluent households are getting more additional dollars in their pocket or purse each year than the fast-growing low-income regions, and they have fewer dependents.

This leads nicely to the other big change in these affluent regions—the lifecycle stage of these consumers. In many of these regions, the number of dependents per wage earner in the household is close to 1 (meaning higher discretionary funds per person) and close to two out of three households contain no one under 19 years of age. In short, these societies have transited from being family households to being either working-age empty nesters or retired households. The reader is reminded that the working age now extends to age 70 in these regions. This transition in life stage has significant implications for the range of products and services that will be sought, as well as the manner in which they will be purchased. Looking first at the range of products and services, there will be little growth in what one might regard as the traditional household products (for example, household cleaning products), as these are already at saturation, with every household able to afford all they need for some considerable time, and there is relatively little growth in the number of households. For obvious reasons (declining number of children), the demand for education services will probably decline or show little growth as well. The growth areas of expenditure will be self-actualisation products and services. This will drive increased demand for personal care products, wellness, recreation (which is part of wellness), communications, health maintenance and health care. In addition, total savings will probably grow at a faster rate because of an apparent change in behaviour that seems to be emerging where the higher-income households (with an income in excess of US$100,000 per annum) reduce their propensity to spend on most categories except housing and health. In effect, they have decided they have got enough things and would rather save the money. For that reason, the luxury products segment, which has grown in line with the increased number of affluent households, may now grow at a slower relative rate. But do note, the number of affluent households continues to increase rapidly. In 2012, there are an estimated 112 million households in these three regions with an income in excess of US$100,000; this is projected to increase to 155 million by 2032. For the same reason, the savings and pension market might well experience accelerated growth. The biggest competitor to this is, of course, potential demand for health services. This may not be a major issue as in all these regions there is generally a fairly good public health service available and the existing spend per condition is already relatively high. Clearly, the more affluent may well seek a higher standard of care at their own expense.

The other change that is occurring in these regions is how they shop. It must be remembered that all countries in these regions have a good

educational history and therefore a very high proportion of the households and populations are capable consumers, in particular, technologically capable. Furthermore, it is not restricted to the young in these
countries. A household consisting of persons over the age of 60 has a very
high probability of having a computer and Internet connection. With
that, the growth of online shopping, be it for products (clothing, particularly, and, increasingly, food) or services (such as holidays), is expected
to continue and with that the range of inventory and prices that they can
review, as well as the location of that inventory changes dramatically. The
traditional retail environment is clearly going to change in nature over
the next 20 years, as it has been in fact over the last 10 years.

So, to conclude in terms of the older affluent regions, the expectation is that the consumer markets will continue to grow but will
change in composition of products and services as well as where they are
sold through. They will also continue to be the major consumer markets
of the world.

Finally, one should factor in the potential growth in these parts of
the world of manufacturing. The increasing use of robotics and new
developments, such as 3D printing, change the very cost dynamics of
manufacturing and make it possible for it to take place closer to where
the market is. For that reason, it may not be long before shirts manu-
factured by machines only are made and sold in these parts of the world.
Similarly, the high education standard of these countries means that they
will be able to operate and use more sophisticated technology more
widely, giving another manufacturing advantage. Basically, it is indicated
that the popular assumption that manufacturing has left these regions for
good may not be correct and one should consider the possibility of these
countries fulfilling new roles, possibly at the expense of other regions in
the world, as discussed below. This will probably have a positive impact
on GDP growth.

Eastern Europe

The next group to examine is Eastern Europe. It actually has not
received as much attention as it perhaps deserved in the past decade. In
terms of total consumer spending, it is 86 percent of the size of the

Chinese consumer market. Furthermore, it has advantage in the quality of the spend—63 percent of the households in this region have an annual income in excess of US$15,000. Which means the profit potential is greater. In terms of population it is 7 percent of the population in the 74 countries covered by this book decreasing marginally to 6 percent over the next 20 years and accounts for 6 percent of all consumer spending, which is quite a nice ratio. By way of comparison China accounts for 7 percent of the world's consumer spending, with 23 percent of the world's population. The changes that are going to occur here are first the total population continues to age and decline in absolute size very marginally in number. It has a relatively low birth rate and a decreasing number of women of child-bearing age so this scenario is unlikely to change in the next 20 years. However, the productivity per worker is showing strong growth and with that household incomes are expected to grow quite strongly. In total, consumer spending is projected to grow by 41 percent in absolute terms over the next 20 years (1.7 percent per annum).

A significant factor that should be considered in terms of this region is that it has a well-educated labour force albeit one declining in size, which is cheaper to employ than Western European worker. As such, one might expect significant increases in investment in this region for manufacturing purposes for products intended particularly for the western European market. The logistical advantage combined with the increasing cost competitiveness relative to China particularly would encourage this to happen. Already, many countries in this region have a return per US$1 wage close to that of China.

Overall, Eastern Europe can be considered as a region that will show quite solid economic growth and with that, ever more affluent consumers. Initially, it will be a manufacturing hub for Western Europe and, increasingly, over time, a consumer market in its own right.

South America

South America is the classic example where perceptions about the consumer need to change quite dramatically. The perception that has formed is that this is a very young part of the world. This is with good reason because, even in 2012, an estimated 41 percent of the population in this region is under the age of 25 years. However, like everywhere else in the world, the population is getting older as the number of births decline. By 2032, the proportion of the population under 25 is expected to have declined to 31 percent. This is quite a significant change in the profile of the population, moving away from households which are largely young children to increasingly older-person households, or households with older children. In short, middle age is coming to South America.

At the same time, it is expected to continue to quietly grow its affluence. It will achieve this because it has a relatively good education standard for its workforce and, more to the point, it is expected to continue to improve. With that, productivity per worker is expected to grow at 1.9 percent per annum, giving in absolute lift of 50 percent over the next two decades. This is expected to flow through to household incomes and consequently these will grow at about 1.78 percent per annum. However, that is on a base of an average household income in 2012 of US$28,000. By 2032, it is expected that the average household will have an income of US$40,000, placing them effectively in the middle income part of the world. (US$40,000 is the average household income across all 74 countries included in the study.) So, sadly, the young vibrant South America is potentially becoming middle class middle income. In total, in 2012, this region will account for 7 percent of all consumer expenditure of the countries covered, increasing marginally to 8 percent by 2032. This is in the context of containing 8 percent of total population; so, like Eastern Europe, it is achieving its weight.

The interesting aspect of this region is that it is one of the regions which successfully transits through the 200 level on the education index, the point at which it would appear that the productivity of workers can grow at a faster rate. This is important because at the same time the total labour force showing relatively little growth. It is estimated to be 200 million persons in 2012, increasing to 235 million by 2032. As such, the growth of the total GDP of these economies increasingly has to be a function of increased productivity per worker rather than increased number of workers, and as explained in the previous paragraph the expectation is that the workforce productivity will grow at an average rate of 1.9 percent per annum over the next 20 years. This is not a brilliant growth rate compared with other regions of the world, but at least it is a strong rate.

Overall, the households in this region are still largely family households. In 2012, three out of four households have a child under the age of 19, but by 2032, this will have reduced to two out of four, and with that there will be a change in the pattern of consumption as it moves away from being a family market to increasingly working age empty nester market the nature of whose demand has been described in greater detail when discussing the affluent regions of the world. It should also be remembered that while the growth rates of this part of the world may not be spectacular, it is still nonetheless a middle income region and with that able to afford a higher-quality product and provide for the manufacturers of such products reasonable profit opportunity.

Finally, just as the increasing cost and reducing supply of labour in China will cause ripples within Eastern Europe, so, too, would have impacts on this part of the world. Remember, North America is a significant 29 percent of all consumer spending in the world, and certainly Mexico with its cost of labour increasing competitive to that of China and its close access to the North American market will probably benefit from this change.

Developing Asia

There are really two Developing Asias. One consists of South Asia, which is Pakistan and Bangladesh and probably Sri Lanka. It would also include India, except that it is being treated as a region in its own right. These three countries have relatively large populations and are quite poor. Over half the population is under the age of 25 and, given that there is no significant drop in birth rate and an increasing number of women of childbearing age, total births will show no decline over the next 20 years. As a consequence, the number of people of working age continue to increase over the next 20 years and, with that, assuming current levels of employment are maintained, so is the overall labour force. For example, the projection for Pakistan indicates a 57 percent increase in the number of employed people. This, of course, provides the economy with a growth engine, which is good. However, the huge number of children per household means that even through to 2032 the average wage earner in the household is supporting over 1.5 persons in addition to themselves. This limits the ability of the household to save and also, of course, means a lower income per capita. It also limits the resources available per child for education.

Average household income in Bangladesh and Pakistan is quite low and, with a relatively poor education scenario, incomes are not expected to grow significantly over the next two decades. The biggest issue facing these countries is really one of employment. A significant increase in the labour force is only useful for the economy if all these people can be kept employed. However, as discussed later in the context of India, because a large proportion of the labour force has little or no education, the probability of this being achieved is under threat from the growth in the use of robots pretty much anywhere in the world. Education, therefore, is probably one of the most critical variables for the future survival, let alone success, of these countries.

The rest of Developing Asia encompasses Indonesia, Malaysia, Philippines, Thailand, Vietnam, and Cambodia. To some extent, these countries have almost been forgotten because the focus has been on China and India while, at the same time, these countries have been relatively stable politically and economically and therefore off people's radar. It is quite a diverse group of countries, in that Malaysia is probably on the cusp between Developing Countries and Developed Countries. It has an average household income of US$22,000, making it by far the most affluent of this set. The other countries in this region have a lower average household income, but all have quite good prospects in terms of increased affluence. In aggregate, their population will increase by 16 percent over the next 20 years, which is much lower than the growth rate of the previous two decades and reflects the maturing of these populations. 45 percent are under the age of 25 in 2012, and this is projected to reduce 37 percent by 2032. This is quite a significant change. However, it does not translate into a rapidly growing labour force, and the reason for that is that female participation rates in most (but not all) of these countries is quite low and has remained so in spite of significant improvements in education by gender.

The good news in terms of these economies is that they do have a relatively high standard of education, and it is improving quite rapidly, such that by 2032 only Vietnam will still be below the 200 index mark. Between now and 2032, Indonesia and Thailand will pass that level. This means that the productivity of workers in these countries can be expected to grow faster than before. In fact, this region is projected to achieve one of the highest gains in productivity of any covered in this book. As a consequence, household incomes can also be expected to increase quite rapidly. One of the factors driving this lift in incomes is a potential shift of manufacturing to this region from China as the supply side of labour in that country gets worse. Indonesia is already an obvious choice for locating new manufacturing facilities, given its large popu- lation, ports, and relative political stability. Thailand and Malaysia are similarly appealing. So, the changes in China in terms of supply of labour (and cost) are probably very good news for these economies and ulti- mately these consumers.

In terms of consumption, this population is still quite young and the majority of households (80 percent) still have children under the age of 19 and, typically, there are 1.5 or more dependents per wage earner. So, they are very much family households and the consumption will reflect that. It is only at the top end of the income scale that there is a movement to more discretionary nonfamily expenditure. In aggregate, this region accounts for just 3 percent of the total household expenditure across the 74 countries covered in this book. The picture changes only marginally over the next 20 years. This compares with the region accounting for 15 percent of population.

North Africa and the Middle East

This is an area of the world has a rapidly growing population (at 1.8 percent per annum it is the highest of any region by a significant margin), with 53 percent of the population currently under the age of

25, which only reduces marginally to 48 percent by 2032. Household size is 4.6 and the number of dependents per wage earner is over two. So, collectively, the typical household in this part of the world is a young family household. Education standard overall is quite competitive and closely matches that of China and South America. This means the productivity per worker is also quite high, at US$16,000.

In terms of consumer spending, it is not a particularly important market because while the population is quite large, the majority of them are children and not yet participating in the economy. As such the total spending by households in this part of the region is just 2.7 percent of the total spending of all households in the regions covered by this book, and this is not expected to change significantly by 2032. However, it might be noted that while the total spending may not be particularly significant it is an area that has a very uneven distribution in terms of household income and, as a result, does have pockets of significant wealth. At present, it has more households with an income in excess of US$100,000 than does China.

Probably the biggest issue facing this region is its rapidly growing labour force. From 125 million in 2012, it is projected to reach 193 million by 2032. This is a significant increase driven not by a change in participation rates but simply a growth in the number of people of working age. Therefore, this potential increase in the size of the labour force is inevitable given that many of the entrants to the labour force are already alive. But the question is, while they are relatively well educated, will there be enough investment in the region to create jobs for these people? Theoretically, there should be, as parts of this region also have easy access to the key consumer markets of Western Europe. But, in reality, political uncertainty around this region in 2012 would indicate that there might be some in hesitation about investing there. That would cause unemployment, which is not desirable from both a sociological point of view and a political stability point of view.

India

The one thing that India is not short of is people. The current slow decline in the propensity to have children is offset by the increasing number of women of childbearing age, which means that total births will continue at about 25 million people a year for the next 20 years. Unless India introduces dramatic controls on births, this outcome is inevitable. It means that India's young population is sustained in absolute size for the next two decades at least. The reader is reminded that while the under-30 age groups maintain (but not increase) their size, it is the 30 years and above age groups that are now increasing in size.

Now, the claim for India is that all these young people will translate into a growing workforce, which in turn will grow the economy. This, of course, is the wrong objective. It should not be growing the economy but rather growing the affluence of individuals within the economy. That would be a much more desirable outcome. But can India lift the affluence of its population? The critical point here is the ability of all these young people entering the labour force to be more productive, or even gain employment. This in turn is a function of, not surprisingly, education. At the present moment, only an estimated 81 percent of 6- to 12-year-olds go to school, and this has an obvious knock-on effect in terms of the proportion of the slightly older population going to secondary school and then onto vocational and tertiary. Now, the trend is extremely good and it is most likely that within the next decade if not sooner, 100 percent of young children will get to primary school. As a result, by 2032, a significant proportion of secondary school students will have graduated and entered the labour force. It is estimated that the number of secondary school educated people in the labour force of India will increase from 24 percent to 49 percent over the next two decades. This is a desirable trend because it does translate into the ability to be employed and for the population to be able to support itself to a more desirable standard. However, the issue is this. Education takes time to translate into a benefit for the society. Individuals need to first complete their education then enter the labour force, which, from age 5 to age 18, is 13 years before the benefit is felt. India has an advantage in that, in 2032, 49 percent of the labour force will have entered sometime after today, which means that it can rejuvenate its labour force in this manner.

However, is it quick enough? The encroachment of robotics and generally improved automation of manufacturing processes means that the demand for a relatively low-educated labour force (which is 40 percent of India's labour force by 2032) is going to decline on a global basis, and this means the ability to keep these people employed is also under pressure. If India is not able to achieve a significant improvement in education facilities and cannot keep these people employed, then it is extremely likely to be confronting political problems over the next two decades.

As mentioned, India is, of course, quite a young country and, with that, most households have someone under the age of 19 in them. In fact, they typically have three people under the age of 19 in them, and in a household with only 1.7 wage earners. This means that India has a very high dependency ratio and, as a result, per capita incomes are actually quite low. It must be remembered that each person in the household represents a fixed cost of some sort, and therefore, the ability of the household to save in a scenario in which there are four people in the household is significantly constrained. This means a household cannot save for additional or better education, unexpected health issues, or generally improving their quality of life.

The other issue for India is perhaps not realising its growth potential, because a significant proportion of its labour force simply does not participate in the economy. That is, adult females. In most countries, over 50 percent of females are employed. In India, it is just 39 percent. If India could change its attitude toward female employment (and at the same time make education available to females on a wider basis), then it could grow its labour force quite significantly—provided, of course, employment opportunities were available to them.

But under the present scenario with a relatively low proportion of the population actually engaged in the economy (37 percent) the income of households is also rather low. In 2012, the average household income is estimated at US$5,724 with a household size of 4.7 persons. In fact, an estimated 79 percent of households are living on less than US $7,500 per annum, which is the equivalent of US$4 per person per day. However, with expected growth in education and workers per household, real average household income should reach US$11,900 per annum by 2032. Because of the large family size, the majority of this income will be spent and actual saving rates will continue to be quite low. However, even though there is a high propensity to spend, India in total, while representing 21 percent of the total population in the countries covered by this book, is just 3 percent of total household expenditure. This proportion will grow, but only marginally, such that it is 5 percent by 2032. So, in the context of global consumer markets, India is and will remain relatively unimportant. It will represent very large volumes but with low revenue per customer. This is, of course, at odds with the claims by many of the booming middle class in India. One suspects it is really a question of definition. In a recently published study it was claimed that 28 percent of India's population is now middle class. Based on the publicly available data on the distribution of households by income and the proportion of the GDP that is private consumption expenditure, this means a household with an income of US$6,250 and a household size of 4.5 persons (which means US$3.80 per person per day) is middle class. Clearly there are different perceptions about what is middle class, as explained earlier.

In conclusion on India, it is really important to stress that the future of this country and its potential importance to the world depends very much on the ability to get the education aspects sorted quickly. As mentioned, by 2032, an estimated 49 percent of the labour force in that year would have entered sometime after today. So, the country has an opportunity to accelerate the education standard of its labour force. But, if it doesn't move quickly on this, then that opportunity will disappear, and never again will India be able to so quickly upgrade its skill set. Failure to do this limits productivity and earning ability and ultimately the standard of life of its residents, which affects political stability.

China

Finally, China, which has been the focus of so much attention over the last decade. Clearly, China has done an incredible job in terms of improving the standard of living of its citizens and the overall strength of the economy. From a demographic point of view, much of this improvement can be traced to the decision to implement the one-child policy. Irrespective of one's perceptions about the acceptability of such a social policy, it has to be agreed that by implementing it and reducing the number of children being brought into the world each year, China has first been able to educate them to increasingly good standard, then second, is reasonably sure of providing employment when they reach adult life. Without the improvement in education, it is considered that much of the other improvements in China would not have been achieved. Productivity per worker could not have grown, because as workers, they would not have been able to use the more sophisticated equipment and machinery associated with higher educated labour (e.g., the use of computers).

The combination of improved education and hence productivity per worker, combined with the growing workforce and a relaxing political environment, meant that China was able to achieve an average growth rate in its total real GDP of 10.5 percent per annum between 2002 and 2011. Real productivity per worker during that period increased at an average growth rate of 10.1 percent per annum, in line with the improving overall education standard of the workforce. At the same time, the number of employed persons grew at an average rate of 2.4 million per annum.

Ironically, and perhaps not appreciated by many, this strength in the overall economy and productivity per worker did not initially flow over to the households themselves. For the period 2000 to 2005, the private consumption share of the economy (and by implication wages) showed no real growth at all. In short, the people did not benefit from the growth of the overall economy through to 2005. Between 2002 and 2005, the private consumption share of the GDP declined from 41 percent to 33 percent, meaning that total household expenditure grew by 6.4 percent per annum, while the overall economy grew at 11.2 percent per annum in real terms. After 2005, this changed and household incomes have moved upwards in line with the total economy (10.2 percent per annum) and that, of course, has resulted in a significant improvement in the overall affluence of households and of course the growth of the more affluent segment.

However, a very critical number of issues have occurred or are occurring from 2012 through 2032 that impact the future projection of the economy. Collectively, they argue that total GDP would achieve an average annual growth rate of 4.1 percent for the next decade, then 2.7 percent for the decade after that to 2032. There are good reasons for believing that this will be the case but, more important, it is necessary to stress that this slower growth rate is very different from a negative growth rate. Many tend to perceive that any growth rate below 8 percent per annum is bad news. That is not the case for China, as, while the growth rate will slow, the population is projected to decline and the workforce is now declining, so while the total economy might be growing at a slower rate, the affluence of the individual participant in the economy is still growing at quite a good rate. An increasing proportion of the economy is moving across to the labour force in the form of increased wages driven by a combination of a shortage of labour as well as an overt government policy to increase the share of the economy that goes to the private sector. So, while the economy might only grow at an average rate of 4.1 percent per annum for the next decade, real household incomes are projected to grow at 6.0 percent, which means they increase by 79 percent in real terms in the next 10 years, and nearly triple from their 2012 level by 2032. This will have significant implications for the distribution of households by income, which, in turn, impacts the consumer market value of China.

Before we look at the overall value of the consumer market in China, it is necessary to digress to some of the other demographic changes taking place in China. As mentioned earlier, China has a relatively old population. Already, over half the households in China no longer contain someone under the age of 19; this proportion will increase to nearly two-thirds of households by 2032. That means that average household size will drop from 3.11 persons to 3.0, and with that, a growth in per household per capita incomes. In fact, the future changes in the demographics of China are quite dramatic. Over the next 20 years, the number of people under the age of 24 will decline in absolute number by 123 million. This has to have implications for a wide range of products and services aimed at the youth and child markets. The family stage household also declines in number, and the working-age empty nester stage typically, 45 through to 64 years of age, shows only marginal growth. The real growth segment demographically in China is the aged. At the present moment, China accounts for one in four people in the world over the age of 65 and, by 2032, will have one in three. In total, the number of people over age 64 in China will double in 20 years.

This change in the age profile of the population has in part predicated the growth in consumer spending. As household size became smaller (i.e., fewer dependents), the per capita household income has gone up quite rapidly. That, combined with people entering a stage in life where the household is already well equipped (washing machine, refrigerator, etc.), means that there has been a rapid increase in the household's more discretionary funds, which can be spent on areas other than family products. To some extent, this is why the Unilever and Procter & Gamble type product is probably not likely to exhibit the same growth rate in the future as it has in the past. Any household who can afford those products are already using them fully, and the number of households is not growing very rapidly anymore. Instead, the growth areas in terms of expenditure are the more self-actualisation or discretionary areas. This includes items such as travel, personal care, wellness, and so on. These are all relatively new areas of consumption in China, for the simple reason that the first wave of better educated consumers is now coming to this stage. These people can interact with the media, are informed of life choices, and are concerned about things like their own health, as well as understanding the nature of different parts of China and the world. So, there are really strong drivers behind this consumption, and it can be expected to continue to grow over the next decade, and probably two decades.

The expected changes in consumer expenditure patterns of China are quite considerable. However, it could be suggested that it has been overstated by some commentators. So, let's pause and look at the facts. Based on the private consumption expenditure component of GDP of the 74 countries covered, in 2012 China accounts for 7.3 percent of all consumer expenditure. It will grow rapidly and, by 2032, will reach 12.3 percent, a significant increase. In fact, that increase will represent 24 percent of the global increase in consumer expenditure between 2012 and 2032, and is almost identical to the proportion of consumer spending growth that is accounted for by North America (22 percent). There is, however, quite a difference in the composition of this expenditure. In North America, 63 percent of this expenditure takes place in households with an income in excess of US$100,000. This increases marginally to 70 percent by 2032. In comparison, for China 57 percent of the expenditure in China takes place in households with an income less than US$15,000 in 2012, and only 7.7 percent is by households with an income in excess of US$50,000. This does change significantly in the next 20 years and, by 2032, an estimated 42 percent of expenditure in China will be by households with an income in excess of US$50,000. At the same time the number of households earning over US$50,000 pa will go from 5.3 million to 54.9 million. This rapid growth in household affluence and spending is clearly a significant opportunity, but it may also cause inflation and the economic growth implications of that.

Problems below the horizon are twofold. First is the rapid ageing of the population. The number of old people will increase dramatically over the next two decades and, with that, so will demand on the health system and the need for provision of care. The one-child policy works nicely for the two (married) children at the bottom of the inverted pyramid in the sense that they inherit from two lots of parents and eight grandparents, but the opposite is not true; the one-childs are not overly keen to support eight grandparents, nor do those children necessarily have the resources to do so. So, whereas the concern in the popular press is often about Japan and its ageing population, in reality, the concern should be about China.

The other problem, which is inevitable but for which there is no obvious solution, is the gender imbalance impact on family formation over the next 20 years. Analysis using data on propensity to be married by age group and the number of people by gender in each group indicates that whereas the problem is relatively small at present, by 2032 there will be 40 million males of marrying age (25 to 39 years of age) who cannot get married simply because of a lack of females aged between 18 and 39 years. Just how this will be handled is difficult to forecast.

To Conclude

Overall, there will be quite a lot of change over the next 20 years. However, change is not the property of one region; they all change in the same general direction and, as a result, while there will be new opportunities and problems as outlined herein, overall, the relative position of the different regions on the key dimensions of age and affluence do not change dramatically. Figure 11.1 is the same as Figure 1.1, except it is the situation as projected for 2032 and demonstrates this point quite strongly.

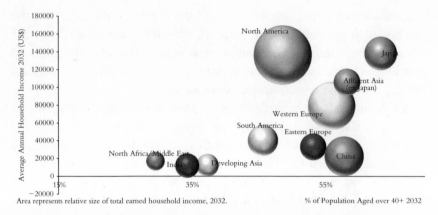

Figure 11.1 The Age and Affluence Profile of the World 2032
Source: Global Demographics Ltd.

So, expect change, but do not assume that it is benefiting one country or region; they are all changing. That is where this book is potentially most useful: It provides a global perspective of the evolving demographic and socioeconomic environment and, in that, shows how all regions have new potentials and offer opportunities. They all have potential risks of differing natures, as well.

About the Author

Dr. Clint Laurent is the founder and managing director of Global Demographics Ltd., formerly Asian Demographics Ltd. Dr. Laurent moved to Hong Kong in 1976, initially with Hong Kong University and then as a director of Price Waterhouse, where he built up a market research and consultancy group. In the following years, Dr. Laurent founded and subsequently sold two leading regional research companies, Asia Market Intelligence Ltd. (now Synovate) and then Asia Studies Ltd., before launching Asian Demographics in 1997.

Asian Demographics developed substantial historical databases of the demographic and socioeconomic profile of the countries of Asia, including China down to county level, and using modelling techniques, provided long-range forecasts of the changing nature of populations, labour force and households, and their income and expenditure patterns. In 2006, Asian Demographics became Global Demographics, and the databases and models were expanded to cover 75 countries, including South and North America, Eastern and Western Europe, and the Middle East, in total representing 79 percent of the world's population and 90 percent of its GDP. Through its Healthcare Subsidiary, the company provides forecasts for disease incidence and treatment affordability. Global Demographics' reports and databases are now used by a wide range of companies throughout the world to assist with their market planning.

Dr. Laurent has a PhD in Marketing and Statistics from Bath University in the United Kingdom.

Index